HANDY REFERENCE

Keyboard shortcuts

F1 .... Launches explanatory text for the current field

Ctrl+N .... Creates a new file

Ctrl+O .... Opens a file

Ctrl+P .... Launches the Print Report or Print Chart dialog

Ctrl+T .... In the Register, toggles between displaying just the top line of transactions, or all lines

Enter or Tab .... Enters a transaction into the Register

Alt+Backspace or Ctrl+Z .... Undoes the last amendment

Ctrl+G .... Jumps back to the most recently edited transaction

Ctrl+Up Arrow .... Moves to the previous transaction in the Register

Ctrl+Down Arrow .... Moves to the next transaction in the Register

Ctrl+Y .... Pastes information from the corresponding field in the previous transaction

Ctrl+S .... Launches the split transaction dialog

Ctrl+M.. Marks a transaction as cleared

Ctrl+K .... Opens the Windows Calculator from within Money

Ctrl+F .... Launches the Find Transactions dialog

Ctrl+D .... Inserts today's date in the Date field

Plus Sign .... Increments numbers/dates

Minus Sign .... Decrements numbers/dates

ABOUT THE SERIES

In easy steps series is developed for time-sensitive people who want results fast. It is designed for quick, easy and effortless learning.

By using the best authors in the field, combined with our in-house expertise in computing, this series is ideal for all computer users. It explains the essentials simply, concisely and clearly - without the unnecessary verbal blurb. We strive to ensure that each book is technically superior, effective for easy learning and offers the best value.

Learn the essentials **in easy steps** - accept no substitutes!

Titles in the series include:

Operating Systems
Windows 95	1-874029-28-8

Applications - Integrated
Microsoft Office	1-874029-37-7
Microsoft Office 97	1-874029-66-0
Microsoft Works	1-874029-41-5
SmartSuite (97)	1-874029-67-9

Applications - General
Access	1-874029-57-1
Excel	1-874029-69-5
PowerPoint	1-874029-63-6
Word	1-874029-39-3
Word 97	1-874029-68-7
WordPerfect	1-874029-59-8

Accounting and Finance
Microsoft Money UK	1-874029-61-X
Quicken UK	1-874029-71-7
Sage Instant Accounting	1-874029-44-X
Sage Sterling for Windows	1-874029-43-1

Internet
CompuServe UK	1-874029-33-4
FrontPage	1-874029-60-1
HTML	1-874029-46-6
Internet Explorer	1-874029-58-X
Internet UK	1-874029-73-3
Netscape Navigator	1-874029-47-4

Graphics and Desktop Publishing
CorelDRAW	1-874029-72-5
PageMaker	1-874029-35-0
PagePlus	1-874029-49-0
Publisher	1-874029-56-3

Development Tools
Visual Basic	1-874029-74-1
Visual J++	1-874029-75-X

For credit card sales and volume discounts Tel: 01926 817999 or EMail: sales@computerstep.com

For international orders and rights Fax: +44 1926 817005 or EMail: sevanti@computerstep.com

EMail your reader comments to: harshad@computerstep.com

Visit our web site at http://www.computerstep.com

MICROSOFT MONEY UK
in easy steps

Stephen Copestake

COMPUTER STEP

In easy steps is an imprint of Computer Step
Southfield Road . Southam
Warwickshire CV33 OFB . England

Tel: 01926 817999 Fax: 01926 817005
http://www.computerstep.com

First published 1997

Notice of Liability
Every effort has been made to ensure that this book contains accurate
and current information. However, Computer Step and the author
shall not be liable for any loss or damage suffered by readers as a
result of any information contained herein.

Trademarks
Microsoft® and Windows® are registered trademarks of Microsoft
Corporation. All other trademarks are acknowledged as belonging to
their respective companies.

Printed and bound in the United Kingdom

ISBN 1-874029-61-X

Contents

1. First Steps 7

Starting Money 8
The Money screen 9
The Navigation Bar 10
Using Money's HELP system 11
    Launching HELP 11
    Using Contents 12
    Using Index 13
    Using Find 13
Running a Product Tour 15
    Running a Product Tour 15
    Terminating a Product Tour 17
Connecting to the MoneyZone 18
    Requirements 18
    Connecting directly from within Money 19
    Connecting from within your browser 20
Using the MoneyZone 21

2. Money Files 23

Files – an overview 24
Creating new files 25
Opening files 26
Backing up files 27
Backup reminders 28
Restoring files 29
Archiving files 31
Exporting files 33
Importing files 35
    Importing a QIF file 35
    Importing a Quicken file 36

3. The Account Register 37

Transactions – an overview 38
Entering transactions 39

AutoComplete 41
Pull-down calendars 42
Pull-down calculators 42
Moving between transactions 43
Categories – an overview 44
Sub-categories 44
Differentiation 44
Using categories/sub-categories 45
Creating categories 46
Creating sub-categories 47
Classifications – an overview 48
Using classifications 49
Applying a classification item 49
Applying a classification sub-item 49
Creating classifications 50
Changing categories/classifications 52
Splits – an overview 53
Creating splits 54
Revising splits – an overview 55
Changing splits 56

4. Accounts 57

Accounts – an overview 58
The Account Manager 59
Creating a new account 60
Opening accounts 63
Opening an account from the Account Manager 63
Opening an account from the Account Register 63
Account editing – an overview 64
Editing account details 65
Closing accounts 66
Deleting accounts 67
Transaction transfers – an overview 68
Transferring money 69
Deleting & voiding – an overview 70
Deleting & voiding in action 71
Print options 72
Printing the Account Register contents 72
Printing lists 72

5. Scheduling Transactions **73**

The Payment Calendar 74
Setting up recurring transactions 76
Amending scheduled entries 78
    Revising scheduled transaction details 78
    Deleting scheduled transactions 79
Dealing with reminders 80
    Using the Payment Calendar reminder 80
    Using the Task Bar reminder 81
Customising reminders 82
    Setting the Payment Calendar notice period 82
    Deactivating the Task Bar reminder 82
Entering scheduled transactions 83
    Using the Payment Calendar's in-built calendar 83
    Multiple selections 84

6. Reconciliation **85**

Reconciliation – an overview 86
Reconciliation – stage one 88
Reconciliation – stage two 91
Reconciliation – stage three 95
Reconciliation – stage four 97
    Editing 98
    Using AutoReconcile 100
    A. If AutoReconcile is successful 100
    B. If AutoReconcile isn't successful 101
    Automatic balancing 102
    The final result 102

7. Reports and Charts **103**

Reports and charts – an overview 104
Report/chart types 106
Creating a standard report 108
Customising reports 110
    Applying a new typeface/type size 112
    Specifying a preset column width 113
    Specifying which transactions are included 114

Getting ready to print reports 115
Report printing 116
Creating a standard chart 117
Customising charts 119
    Applying a chart type 120
    Applying a new typeface/type size 121
    Specifying which transactions are included (A) 122
    Specifying which transactions are included (B) 123
    Other suggestions... 123
    Other changes.. 124
Working with charts 125
    Producing a component display 125
    Direct editing 125
Chart printing 126

8. Planning Wizards 127

Planning Wizards – an overview 128
Running the Mortgage Planner 129
Running the Retirement Planner 136
Running the Savings Calculator 140

9. Home Banking 141

Home Banking – an overview 142
Preparing to sign up.. 143
Signing up for Online Services 145
Paying bills electronically.. 150
Electronic account transfers 152
Writing to Online Services 153
Updating your account 154

Index 155

First Steps

Use this section to start Money (and customise which screen appears when you do so). Learn how to use the Navigation Bar to move between Money screens. Discover how to invoke and use Money's HELP system, then take an interactive Product Tour for more detailed *hands-on* assistance. Finally, connect to the MoneyZone – Microsoft's on-line World Wide Web site – for even more up-to-date help.

Covers

Starting Money 8

The Money screen 9

The Navigation Bar 10

Using Money's HELP system 11

Running a Product Tour 15

Connecting to the MoneyZone 18

Using the MoneyZone 21

Starting Money

To run Money, click the Start button:

Start

in the bottom left-hand corner of the Windows screen. (If the Start button isn't currently visible, move the mouse pointer over the bottom of the screen to make the Windows Task bar appear, *then* click the Start button.)

Now do the following:

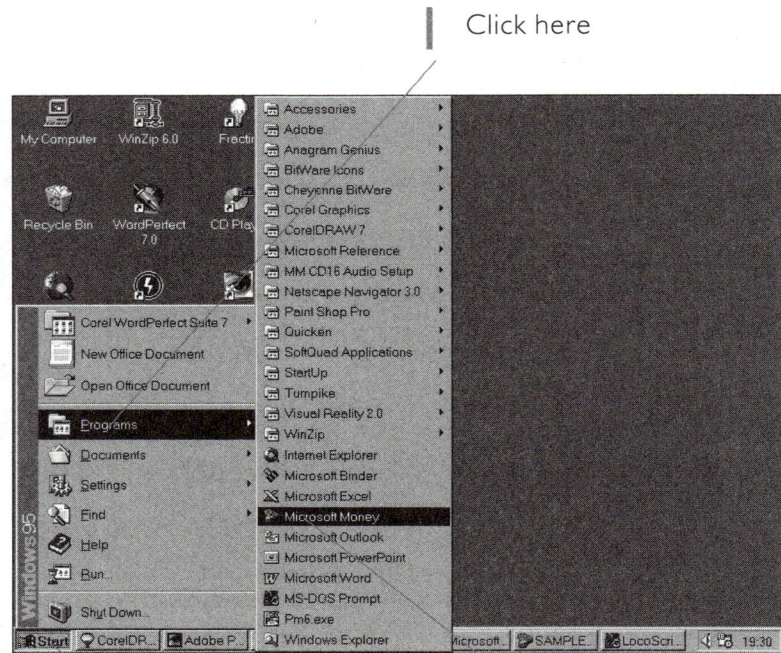

REMEMBER

You can create a shortcut to launch Money directly. See your Windows documentation for how to do this.

Click here

Start button

2 Click here

The Money screen

HANDY TIP

If you want Money to display a different screen at start-up, pull down the Tools menu and click Options. Activate the General tab. In the Display section of the Options dialog, click here:

`Contents`

In the list which launches, select a new screen. Click OK.

By default, when it starts Money displays its Contents screen. This consists of:

- the Navigation Bar, which you can use to jump to another area or launch Money's on-line HELP system – see page 10

- buttons which are links to specific areas (for instance, by clicking the Account Register button you can go immediately to the Register)

- a Tip area

- an on-screen chart area where you can view your favourite charts (varied each day) – see Section 7

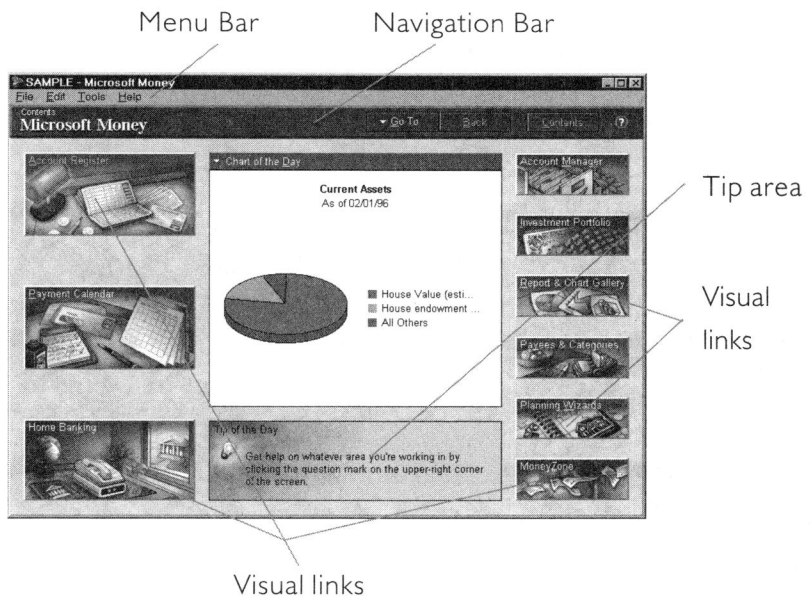

Menu Bar   Navigation Bar

Tip area

Visual links

Visual links

HANDY TIP

To have Money display a new tip, place the mouse pointer over the Tip area. Right-click once. Now do the following:

`Next Tip`

Left-click here

For more information on the Navigation Bar, turn to the following page.

The Navigation Bar

The Navigation Bar is a convenient on-screen area from which you can:

- return to the last used screen

- move specifically to the Contents screen (see page 9 for more information on this)

- go to a 'Favourite' account (see 'Account editing – an overview' in Section 4 for how to mark accounts as Favourites)

- go to an account area (e.g. the Account Register or Account Manager)

Using the Navigation Bar

To jump to the screen you used last, follow step 1 below. To move to the Contents screen, carry out step 2. To go to a Favourite account, follow steps 3 and 4; alternatively, perform steps 3 and 5 to view a specific account area:

REMEMBER

Clicking: ❷ in the top right-hand corner of the Navigation Bar launches Money's HELP system – see the 'Using Money's HELP system' topics which follow.

I Click here   2 Click here

Contents
Microsoft Money   ▾ Go To   Back   Contents   ②

⊗ 1 Household current a/c
▭ 2 John – Credit Card
⊗ 3 John – current a/c
▭ 4 Mary – Credit Card
⊗ 5 Mary – current a/c

⊗ Account Register
⊗ Payment Calendar
⊗ Home Banking
▭ Account Manager
▥ Investment Portfolio
▦ Report and Chart Gallery
⊗ Payees and Categories
⊗ Planning Wizards

3 Click here

4 Click a Favourite account

5 Or click an account area

Using Money's HELP system (1)

Money has an on-line HELP system which allows you to get *context-sensitive* assistance. This is assistance which is tailored to whatever you happen to be doing at the time. For example, if you want assistance with a specific area (e.g. the Account Register), Money will provide it.

Launching HELP

In the Contents screen (or any other area), do the following:

REMEMBER

The HELP window which launches here is specific to the Contents screen. If you follow the procedures discussed here over another area, you get help which is relevant to your current needs...

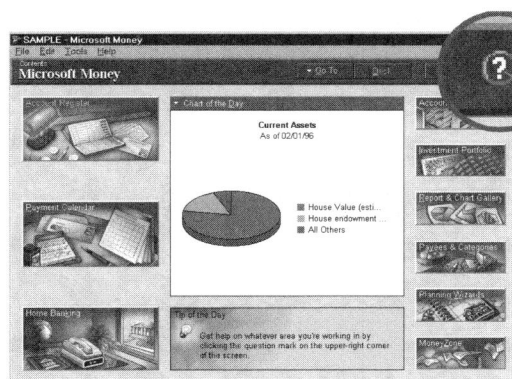

Click here

This is the result:

HANDY TIP

Click any of these buttons to access additional HELP features. (See the following two pages for how to use them.)

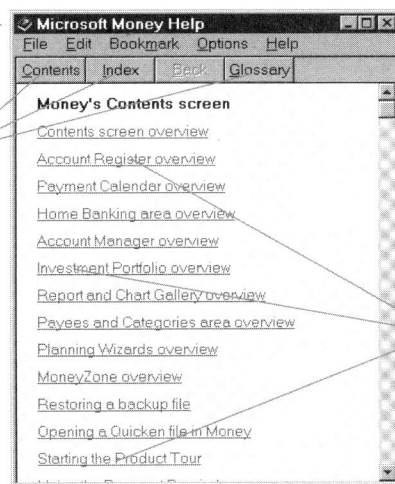

Left-click any entry for access to a specific HELP topic

Using Money's HELP system (2)

You can also launch HELP by using a different route: the Help menu. When you do this, you have access to the following:

- Contents (a list of topics and sub-topics)

- Index (an alphabetical list of topics)

- Find (an indexed HELP database)

Using Contents
Pull down the Help menu and do the following:

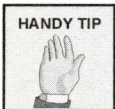

Click here

HANDY TIP **The Contents and Index windows produced here are identical to those produced by clicking the Contents and Index buttons in the context-specific HELP window (see page 11).**

2 Ensure this tab is activated

3 Double-click a topic

4 Double-click a sub-topic

REMEMBER **Re step 5 – you can also press Esc to close a HELP window at any time.**

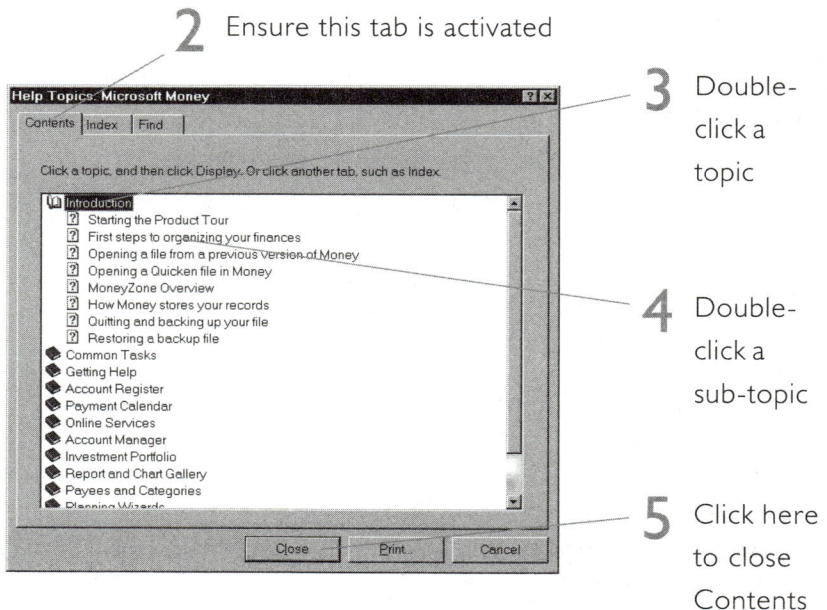

5 Click here to close Contents

Using Money's HELP system (3)

Using Index

Pull down the Help menu and click Help Topics. Now do the following:

HANDY TIP **The Contents and Index windows produced here are identical to those produced by clicking the Contents and Index buttons in the context-specific HELP window (see page 11).**

Ensure this tab is activated

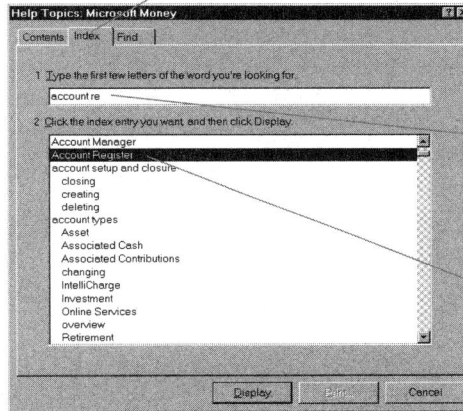

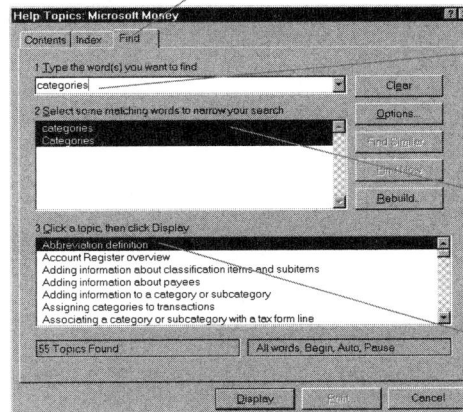

2 Type in a key word/phrase

3 Double-click a topic

REMEMBER **The Find window enables you to locate instances (within the overall Money HELP file) where the key words you enter are associated. Use Find if the other methods don't work.**

Using Find

Pull down the Help menu and click Help Topics. Now do the following:

Ensure this tab is activated

2 Type in a key word/phrase

3 Click a category

4 Double-click a topic

REMEMBER **To close a HELP window at any time, simply press Esc.**

Using Money's HELP system (4)

There is another method you can use to get context-specific assistance within the Contents screen. Do the following:

HANDY TIP

You can also use this method within dialogs. Simply right-click over the dialog field with which you want assistance, then follow step 2.

Right-click any area button

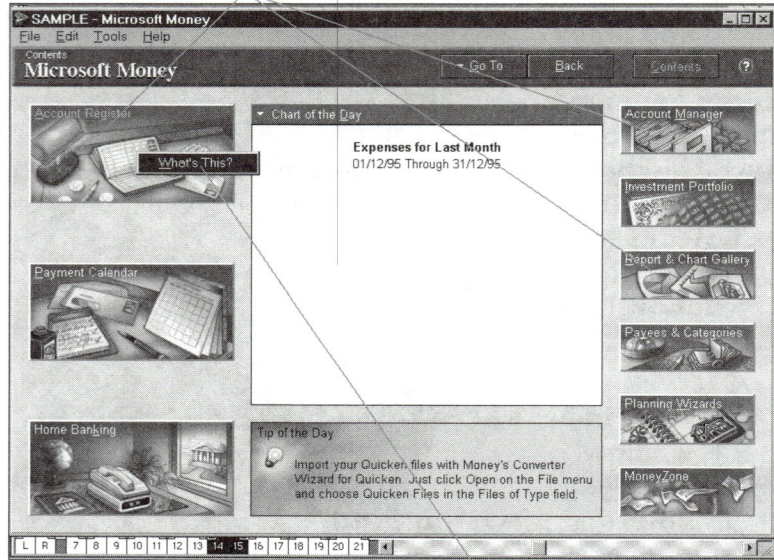

2 Left-click here

Money now launches a special explanatory box:

Click this to go to the Account Register, where you enter all your transactions and balance your accounts. The Account Register is similar to your chequebook. It has a transaction register above and cheques and forms where you can enter transactions below.

When you've finished with it, press Esc. Or click elsewhere in the Money screen.

Running a Product Tour (1)

Money comes with three introductory tours (known as Product Tours):

- for new users

- for users of earlier versions of Money (detailing new features in Money 97)

- for users of Intuit's Quicken

All three are interactive. This means that they draw your attention to specific screen areas, and ask you to do things.

Running a Product Tour

Pull down the Help menu and do the following:

Help
Help Topics
Product Tour
About Microsoft Money...

Click here

REMEMBER **This is the first dialog in the New Users tour.** Note, however, that Money varies the subsequent dialogs according to which tour you've elected to run.

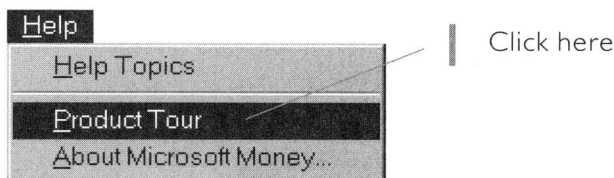

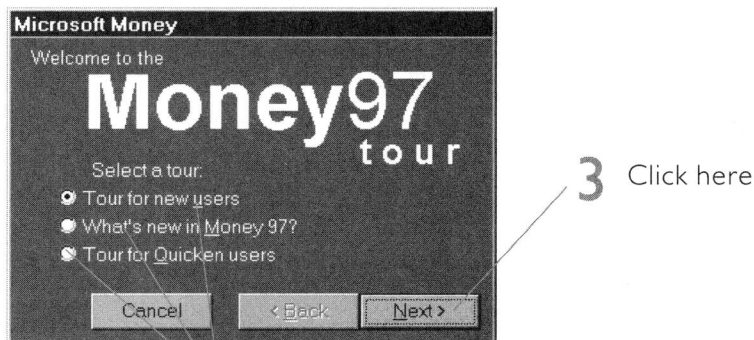

Microsoft Money

Welcome to the

Money97
tour

Select a tour:

- Tour for new users
- What's new in Money 97?
- Tour for Quicken users

Cancel   < Back   Next >

3 Click here

2 Click a Tour

Running a Product Tour (2)

Now do the following:

Money
surrounds
sections of
the screen
that it wants to
draw your attention
to with a red box:

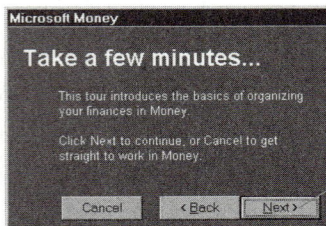

HANDY TIP

Microsoft Money
Take a few minutes...

This tour introduces the basics of organizing
your finances in Money.

Click Next to continue, or Cancel to get
straight to work in Money.

Cancel | < Back | Next >

| Click here

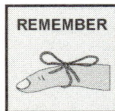

Note that
Money
varies the
dialogs
which appear
according to which
tour you've elected
to run.

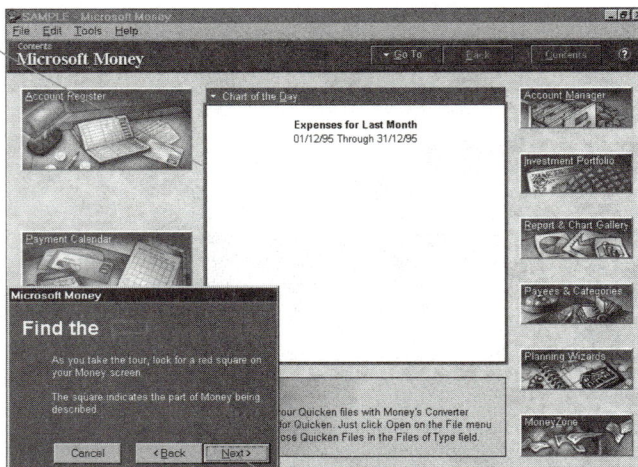

REMEMBER

SAMPLE - Microsoft Money
File Edit Tools Help

Microsoft Money

Go To | Back | Contents | ?

Account Register

Chart of the Day

Expenses for Last Month
01/12/95 Through 31/12/95

Account Manager

Investment Portfolio

Payment Calendar

Report & Chart Gallery

Payees & Categories

Microsoft Money

Find the

As you take the tour, look for a red square on
your Money screen.

The square indicates the part of Money being
described.

Cancel | < Back | Next >

Planning Wizards

MoneyZone

ur Quicken files with Money's Converter
for Quicken. Just click Open on the File menu
ose Quicken Files in the Files of Type field.

2 Click here

In the next instalment, Money provides some instruction:

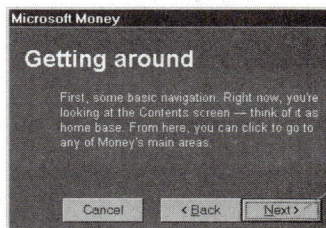

Microsoft Money

Getting around

First, some basic navigation. Right now, you're
looking at the Contents screen — think of it as
home base. From here, you can click to go to
any of Money's main areas.

Cancel | < Back | Next >

3 Click here

Running a Product Tour (3)

Now, whichever Product Tour you're running, follow the on-screen instructions until it's complete.

Terminating a Product Tour

If you want to stop a tour *before* it reaches its natural conclusion, do the following:

 **Money comes with a sample file – Sample.MNY – which you can use to gain experience. If, however, you had your own Money file open before starting the Product Tour, this will appear as a further option here:**

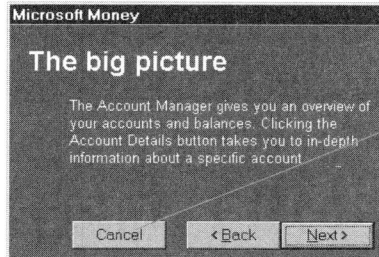

1 Click here (in any Tour window)

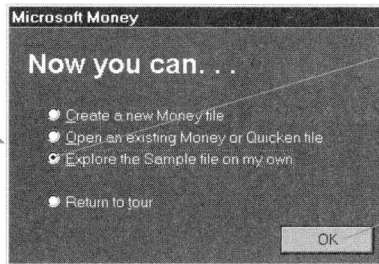

2 Click here

3 Click here

 **If (in step 2) you opted to return to your own Money file rather than Sample.MNY, the window on the right does not appear. Instead, Money reopens your file immediately after step 3.**

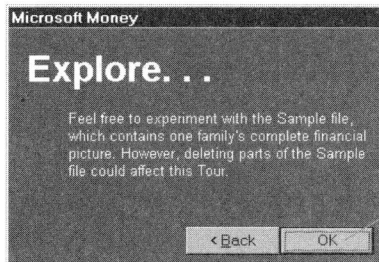

4 Click here

Connecting to the MoneyZone (1)

The MoneyZone is an on-line service which Microsoft maintains in order to provide Money users with immediate (and extremely up-to-date) assistance. Use the MoneyZone to:

- obtain hints/tips relating to your use of Money

- answer any questions you may have about your use of Money

- access up-to-date articles on Money topics. These include:

    – Money itself

    – Home Banking

    – Personal Finance

    – Money Users (lists Frequently Asked Questions – FAQs, for short – and special offers. Also lets you talk directly with other Money users)

Requirements

To use the MoneyZone, you must have:

- a modem connected to your PC

- an ongoing account with an Internet Service provider (e.g. Demon or AOL)

- a compatible Internet browser (for instance, Internet Explorer or Netscape Navigator – the examples shown in this section use these)

Connecting to the MoneyZone (2)

If you meet the requirements set out on page 18, there are two ways you can connect to the MoneyZone.

Connecting directly from within Money

This is the quickest and most convenient method.

REMEMBER

This method of connecting to the MoneyZone requires Money to be open and running at the same time.

First, ensure your PC and modem are active. Open your connection with your service provider. Now switch to Money's Contents screen and do the following:

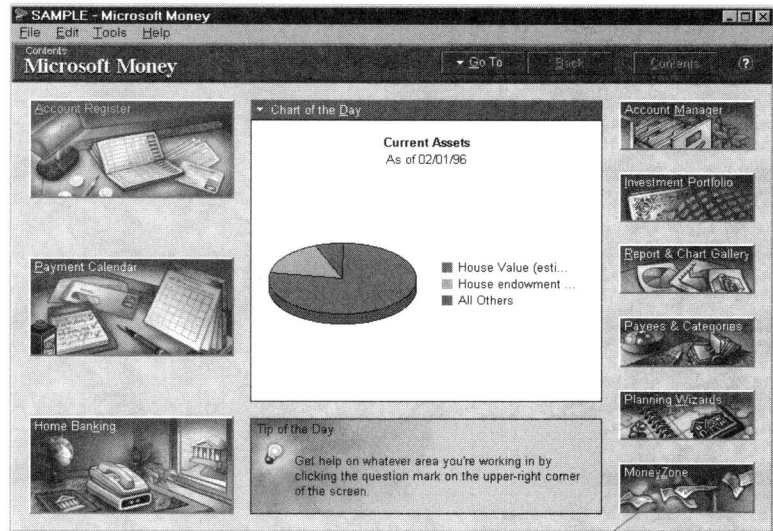

Click here

Two things now happen:

1.   your Internet browser launches

2.   a connection with Money's on-line World Wide Web site is automatically established, and the site is loaded into your browser

For how to use the MoneyZone, see page 21.

Connecting to the MoneyZone (3)

Connecting from within your browser

This method is slightly more long-winded, but still convenient.

REMEMBER **In this method of connecting to the MoneyZone, Money does not have to be open at the same time.**

First, ensure your PC and modem are active. Open your connection with your service provider. Take whatever action is necessary to launch your browser. Now do the following:

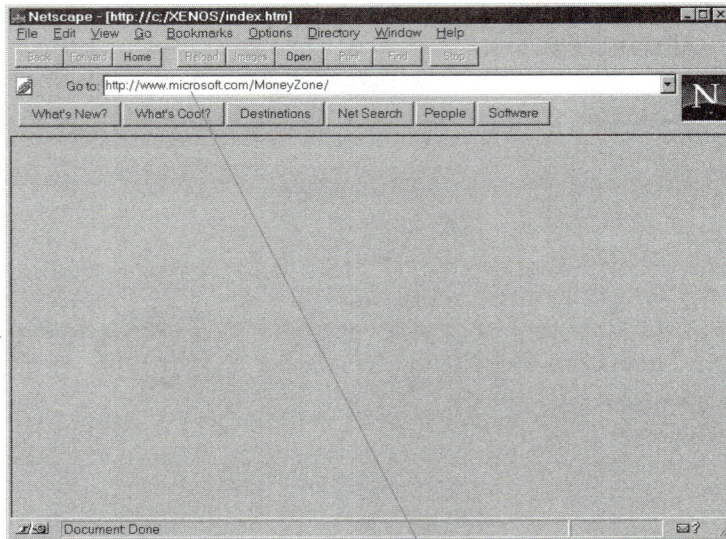

```
Netscape - [http://c:/XENOS/index.htm]
File  Edit  View  Go  Bookmarks  Options  Directory  Window  Help
Back  Forward  Home  Reload  Images  Open  Print  Find  Stop
      Go to: http://www.microsoft.com/MoneyZone/                    N
What's New?  What's Cool?  Destinations  Net Search  People  Software



Document Done
```

REMEMBER **This is Netscape Navigator. If you're using an alternative browser, follow the necessary procedures to open the MoneyZone site. (If you're using Microsoft's Internet Explorer, however, the procedures are identical.)**

Type in the following:
http://www.microsoft.com/
MoneyZone/

Now press Enter; your browser loads the MoneyZone site.

For how to use the MoneyZone, see page 21.

Using the MoneyZone (1)

Whichever method you use to connect to the MoneyZone, this is the result. Do any of the following:

REMEMBER

Here, the MoneyZone Home page is being viewed through Internet Explorer.

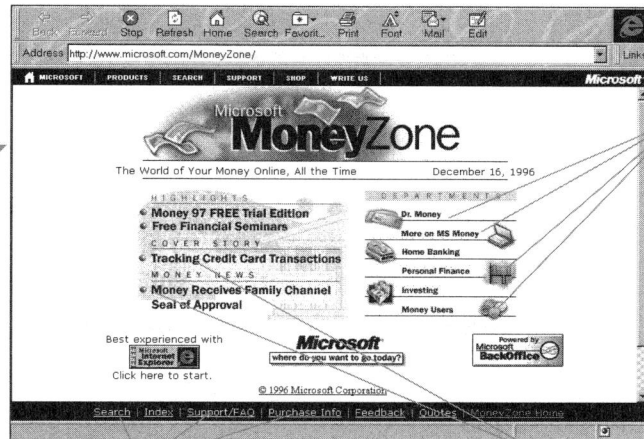

Click any specific feature

Click any of these links

Click any article

The next illustration shows the result of clicking on the Personal Finance feature:

HANDY TIP

To return to the previously viewed MoneyZone page, press Alt+←.

HANDY TIP

To close down your browser at any time, press Alt+F4. Don't forget to terminate your Internet connection, too!

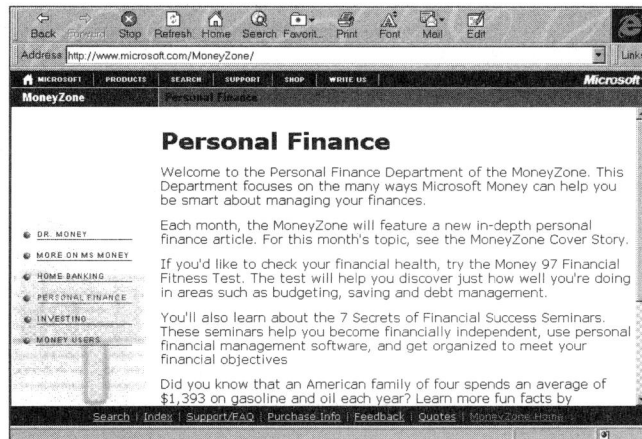

Using the MoneyZone (2)

The following illustrations show further services available from within the MoneyZone:

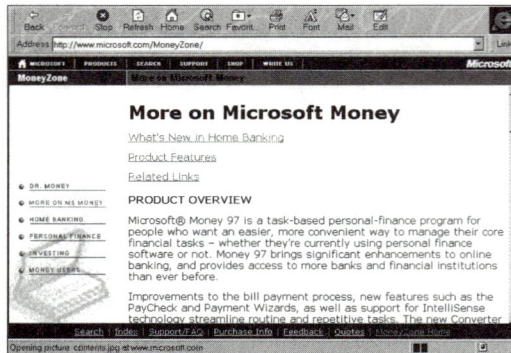

The More on Microsoft Money feature

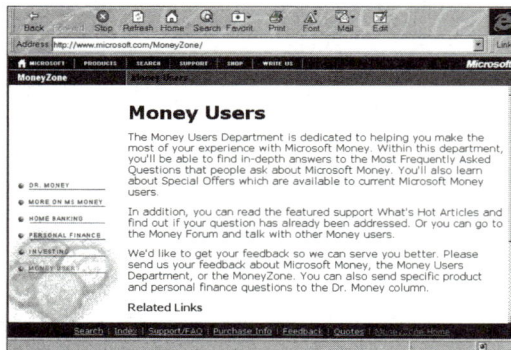

The Money Users feature

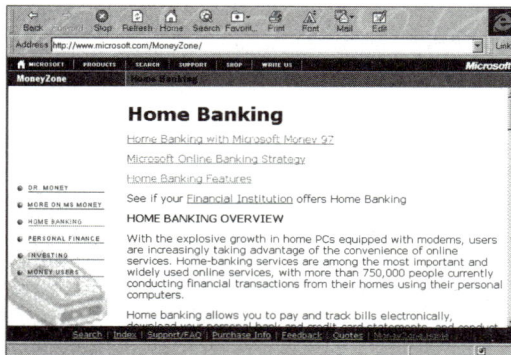

The Home Banking feature – see Section 9 for more information

Money Files

Use this chapter to learn how to work with Money's files. You'll learn about Money's default file, and how to create (and subsequently open) your own. Finally, you'll back up/ archive your files, import third-party data and then export your work for use in other programs.

Covers

Files – an overview 24

Creating new files 25

Opening files 26

Backing up files 27

Backup reminders 28

Restoring files 29

Archiving files 31

Exporting files 33

Importing files 35

Files – an overview

Files are crucial to the way Money works. However, it places a special interpretation on the word. In Money, files are collections of related accounts and transactions. For example, you may have one account which relates to domestic finance, and another which relates to a small business. Since both accounts relate to *you*, Money organises them under the aegis of a single file.

Some more basic Money terminology (these terms are discussed in greater detail later):

***Accounts* are collections of transactions (withdrawals or deposits).**

***The Account Register* is the window through which transactions are entered into an account, and strongly resembles a bank statement.**

Money creates a file automatically – Mine.MNY – when it's installed. Many users never need to create another; however you can do so if you want to (for instance, if you run more than one business it may well be useful to have separate files for each).

You can also:

- back up files

- set automatic backup options

- restore files

- archive files

- export files

- import files

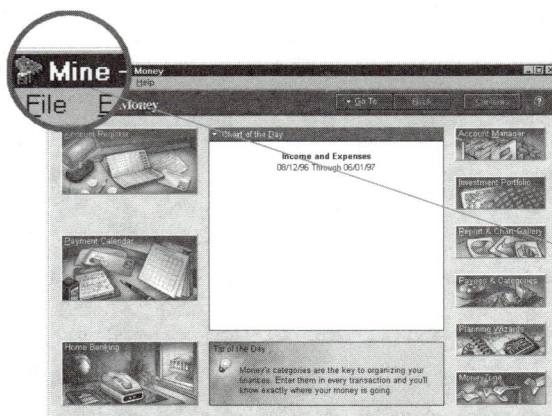

Magnified view of menu bar entry giving details of the underlying file

Creating new files

Money makes it easy to create as many new files (collections of related accounts and transactions) as you need. However, most users find that the file Money creates automatically on installation – Mine.MNY – is more than adequate, for the following reason:

- there is no crossover between files. In other words, if you create a report or chart, it can only be based on a single file. Money treats files as entirely separate entities

Having said this, there are occasions when it is useful – even necessary – to create a new file. You might have businesses whose accounts you want to remain distinct. Or you might wish to create a new account relating to a charity.

Setting up a new file
Pull down the File menu and click New. Now do the following:

REMEMBER

After step 2, Money saves a backup copy of the previously opened file to disk – see pages 27-28 for more information on backing up files.

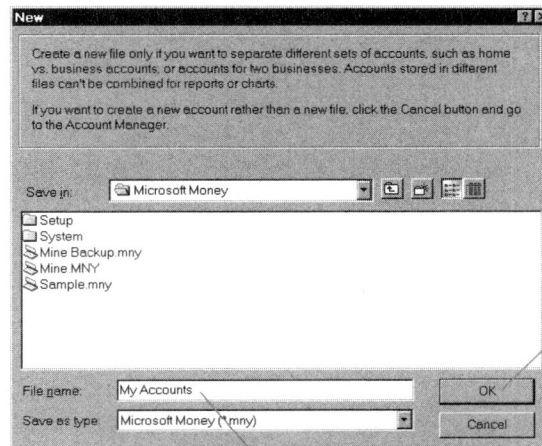

| Name the new file

2 Click here

Opening files

If you've created more than one Money file (perhaps because you run more than one business, or because you wanted to emphasise differing accounting periods), you'll need to open the specific file you need to work with.

Do the following:

```
File
  New...              Ctrl+N
  Open...             Ctrl+O
  Password...

  Backup...
  Restore Backup...
  Archive...

  Import...
  Export...

  Print Setup...
  Print...            Ctrl+P

  Exit                Alt+F4
```

| Click here

HANDY TIP **If you only use the default file Mine.MNY,** you don't need to open it: Money does this for you when you run the program.

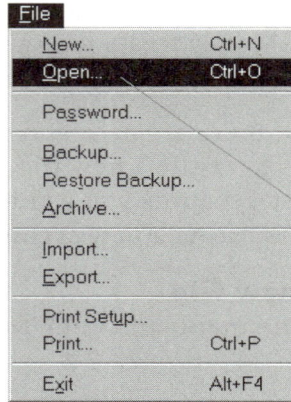

2 Highlight a file

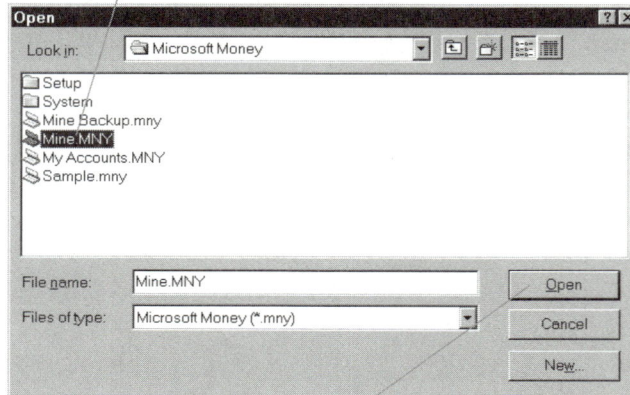

```
Open                                                    ? X
Look in:  [ Microsoft Money        ▼ ]  [±] [🗁] [▦] [▥]
  Setup
  System
  Mine Backup.mny
  Mine.MNY
  My Accounts.MNY
  Sample.mny

File name:     [ Mine.MNY                        ]    [ Open ]
Files of type: [ Microsoft Money (*.mny)      ▼ ]    [ Cancel ]
                                                      [ New... ]
```

3 Click here

Backing up files

HANDY TIP

You should maintain *two* (or more) independent backup copies of your data.

As you work with your Money file(s), it's important to *back up* your work regularly. Backing up is the process of copying data stored on your hard disk to a floppy disk so that, if any hardware- or software-based errors result in data loss, you can get back to the situation you were in before the loss. Money makes carrying out backups easy and convenient.

BEWARE

If you're backing up onto a disk already used for this purpose, Money launches this message:

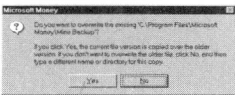

First, open the file you want to back up and place a floppy disk in the relevant drive. Pull down the File menu and carry out the following steps:

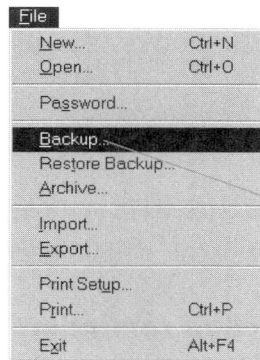

Click here to overwrite the old backup file.

File	
New...	Ctrl+N
Open...	Ctrl+O
Password...	
Backup...	
Restore Backup...	
Archive...	
Import...	
Export...	
Print Setup...	
Print...	Ctrl+P
Exit	Alt+F4

Click here

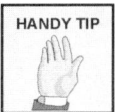

HANDY TIP

You can also back up onto a hard disk, though this isn't recommended.

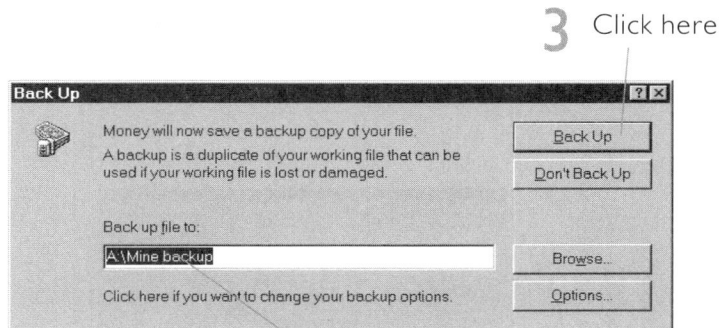

3 Click here

Back Up

Money will now save a backup copy of your file.
A backup is a duplicate of your working file that can be used if your working file is lost or damaged.

Back up file to:

A:\Mine backup

Click here if you want to change your backup options.

Back Up

Don't Back Up

Browse...

Options...

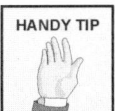

HANDY TIP

Backed up data can easily be copied back (*restored*) to the hard disk – see pages 29-30.

2 Accept the proposed drive/ folder/filename combination, or type in your own

Backup reminders

By default, whenever you do either of the following:

* open a new file

* close Money

Money launches the following message automatically. Do the following to back up the current file:

Money saves your work whenever you make any changes (e.g. enter a transaction or close a dialog), automatically. However, it's still a good idea to let it create a backup copy when you close Money...

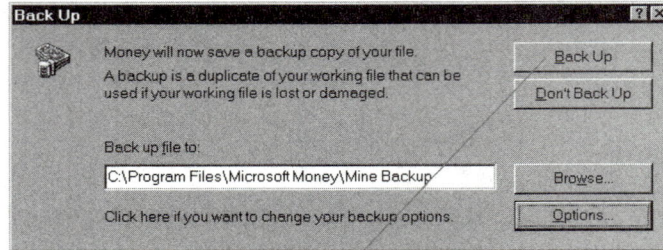

Click here to save an up-to-date copy of the open file to disk

Customising backup reminders

If you want Money to carry out backups (in the circumstances set out above) without your confirmation, or no backups at all, pull down the Tools menu and click Options. Do the following:

Ensure the General tab is active

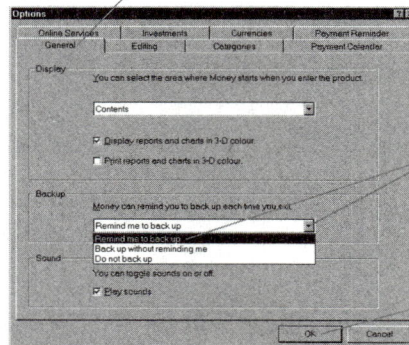

2 Click here; select a backup option

3 Click here

Restoring files (1)

Restoring files is the process of reinstating backed up data (in the case of loss or damage to the original) onto your hard disk. Hopefully, you'll never have to do this. If you do, however, you can take comfort from the fact that Money makes the process very easy.

First, place the backup floppy disk in the relevant drive. (Omit this if the backup file you want to restore is located on your hard disk.) Pull down the File menu and carry out the following steps:

 **Restore can also be used to copy data onto a _different_ hard disk. This equates to a way of transferring data between separate computers. However, both computers must have Money installed on them.**

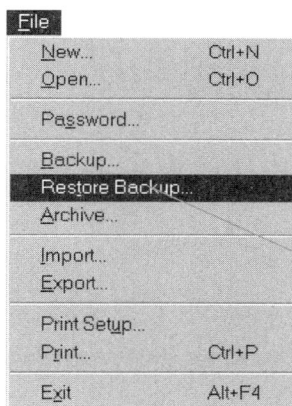

Click here

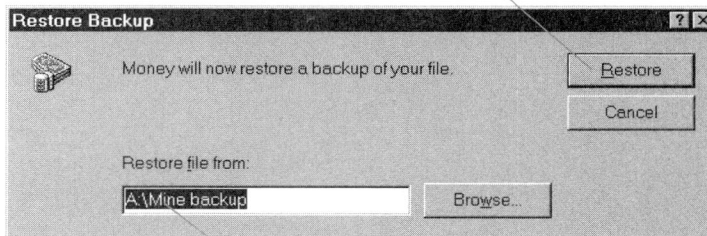

3 Click here

2 Type in the appropriate drive/ folder/filename combination

Restoring files (2)

If it detects a previous version of the file being restored, Money launches this message. Carry out step 1 below if you want to overwrite it with the restored version, or steps 2-4 to have the restored file written to disk as a new file:

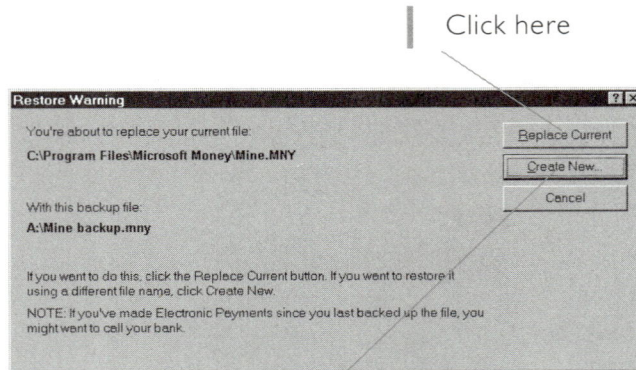

| Click here

Restore Warning `? X`

You're about to replace your current file:

C:\Program Files\Microsoft Money\Mine.MNY

With this backup file:

A:\Mine backup.mny

If you want to do this, click the Replace Current button. If you want to restore it using a different file name, click Create New.

NOTE: If you've made Electronic Payments since you last backed up the file, you might want to call your bank.

Replace Current

Create New...

Cancel

2 Click here

New `? X`

Create a new file only if you want to separate different sets of accounts, such as home vs. business accounts, or accounts for two businesses. Accounts stored in different files can't be combined for reports or charts.

If you want to create a new account rather than a new file, click the Cancel button and go to the Account Manager.

Save in: Microsoft Money

- Setup
- System
- 1996.mny
- Mine Backup.mny
- Mine.MNY
- My Accounts Backup.mny
- My Accounts.MNY
- Sample.mny

File name:

Save as type: Microsoft Money (*.mny)

OK

Cancel

4 Click here

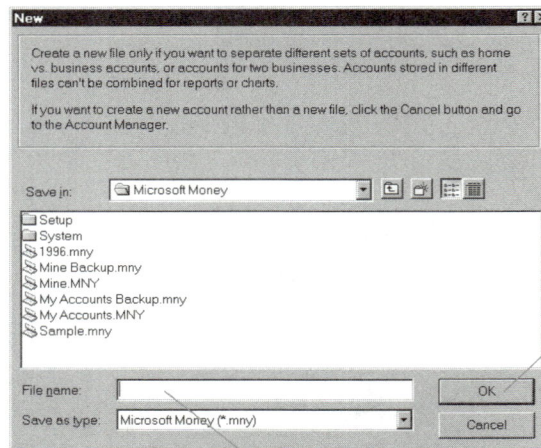

3 Give the restored file a new name

Archiving files (1)

Archiving is a specialised backup procedure. When you archive a file, Money backs it up but, at the same time, it also removes superseded transactions according to criteria you set. Archiving is a housekeeping technique: it ensures that your files do not become too large.

REMEMBER **Archiving is a good way to store accounts which relate to specific years. For example, you might archive selected transactions for 1996 and store them as 1996.MNY.**

When you archive a file, you can specify a date before which files are deleted. Under this overall heading, you can then go on to specify:

- that only reconciled transactions are deleted

- that only cleared/reconciled transactions are deleted

- that no transactions are deleted

- that all transactions are deleted

Creating an archive

First, open the file you want to archive. Pull down the File menu and do the following:

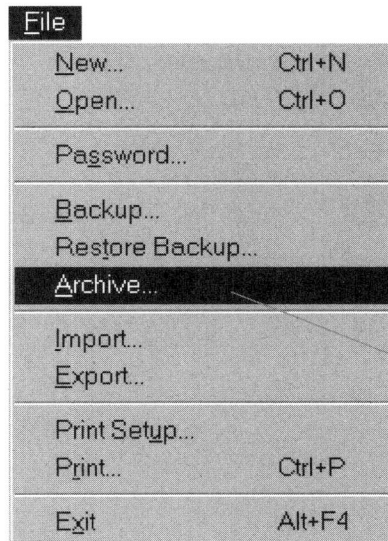

```
File
  New...              Ctrl+N
  Open...             Ctrl+O

  Password...

  Backup...
  Restore Backup...
  Archive...

  Import...
  Export...

  Print Setup...
  Print...            Ctrl+P

  Exit                Alt+F4
```

Click here

Archiving files (2)

Now carry out the following steps:

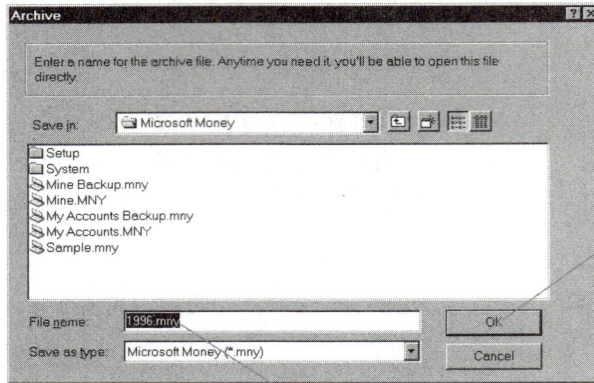

```
Archive                                                          ? X

Enter a name for the archive file. Anytime you need it, you'll be able to open this file
directly.

Save in:    [ Microsoft Money                    ▼] [□] [□] [☲] [▥]

□ Setup
□ System
▧ Mine Backup.mny
▧ Mine.MNY
▧ My Accounts Backup.mny
▧ My Accounts.MNY
▧ Sample.mny

File name:     [1996.mny              ]              [    OK    ]
Save as type:  [Microsoft Money (*.mny)        ▼]  [  Cancel  ]
```

2 Click here

| Name the archive

As the message which launches after step 4 indicates, the archiving process can sometimes be fairly lengthy:

Money is archiving your file and removing unneeded data. If your data file is large, this may take several minutes.

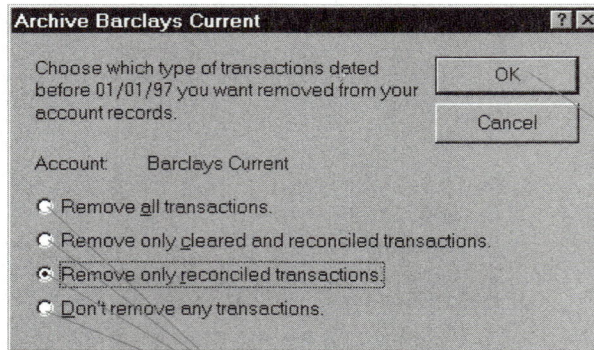

```
Archive Barclays Current                                        ? X

Choose which type of transactions dated        [    OK    ]
before 01/01/97 you want removed from your
account records.                                [  Cancel  ]

Account:    Barclays Current

○ Remove all transactions.
○ Remove only cleared and reconciled transactions.
● Remove only reconciled transactions.
○ Don't remove any transactions.
```

4 Click here

3 Click a deletion option

Exporting files (1)

REMEMBER QIF is a shortened form of 'Quicken Interchange Format'.

REMEMBER See Section 3 for more information on categories and classifications.

Money lets you export your files into either of two formats:

Loose QIF — Money's categories and classifications are translated accurately – suitable for importing accounts into other Money files

Strict QIF — Money's categories and classifications do not translate completely – suitable for importing into other programs such as Quicken

Exporting a file

Open the file you want to export. Pull down the File menu and click Export. Now do the following:

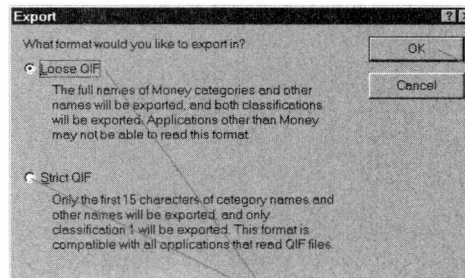

2 Click here

| Click a format

3 Name the exported file

REMEMBER Re step 3 – ensure the name you allocate has the following suffix: .QIF

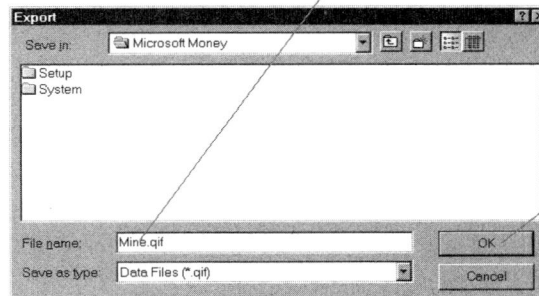

4 Click here

Exporting files (2)

Now do the following:

2 Click here

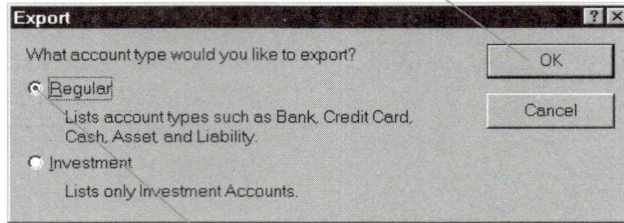

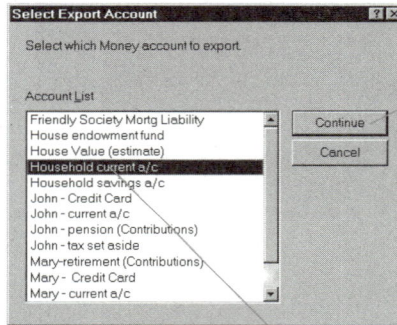

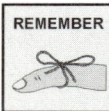

**Re step 3 –
see
Section 4
for more
information on
accounts.**

4 Click here

3 Select an account

5 Click here

Importing files (1)

You can import two principal kinds of files into Money:

- QIF files previously exported from Money (or other programs)

- native Quicken files

Both options translate the files in the process.

Importing a QIF file

Open the file into which you want the QIF file inserted. Pull down the File menu and click Import. Carry out the following steps:

Re steps 4 and 5 – Money needs to know where the accounts in the file being imported should be placed in the host file. This dialog appears as many times as there are imported accounts. Follow steps 4-5 as often as necessary.

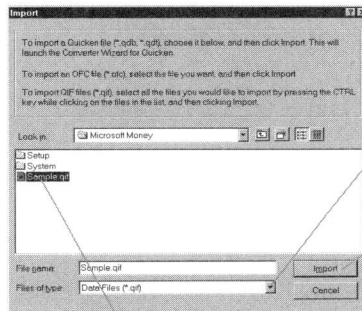

I Click here; select Data Files (*.qif)

3 Click here

2 Select a QIF file

After you've carried out step 5 for the last time, Money launches this message:

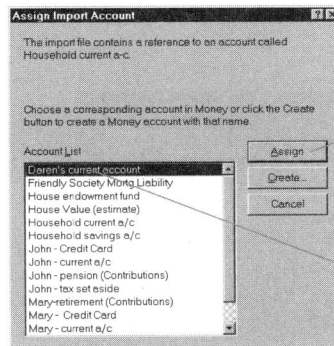

5 Click here

4 Select a host account

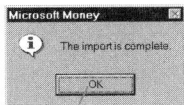

Click here

Importing files (2)

Importing a Quicken file

Open the Money file into which you want the Quicken file inserted. Pull down the File menu and click Import. Carry out the following steps:

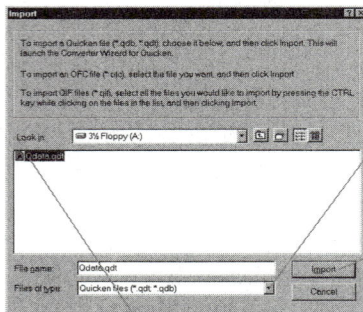

1 Click here; select Quicken files (*.qdt *.qdb)

3 Click here

2 Select a Quicken file

 REMEMBER

After step 4, Money launches two extra dialogs. Do the following:

Name the file

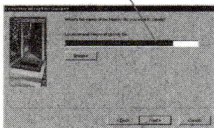

Click here

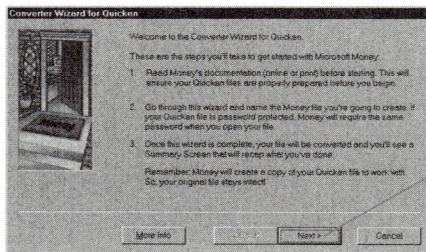

4 Click here

In the next, no action is required:

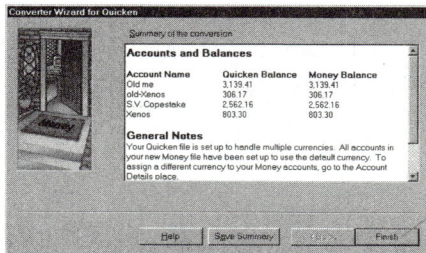

5 Click here

Finally, carry out step 5.

The Account Register

Use this chapter to learn how to enter transactions into the Account Register, and move between them. You'll apply categories/sub-categories and classifications to transactions, and discover how to create your own. Finally, you'll 'split' transactions, to make your accounts even more accurate.

Covers

Transactions – an overview 38

Entering transactions 39

Moving between transactions 43

Categories – an overview 44

Using categories/sub-categories 45

Creating categories 46

Creating sub-categories 47

Classifications – an overview 48

Using classifications 49

Creating classifications 50

Changing categories/classifications 52

Splits – an overview 53

Creating splits 54

Revising splits – an overview 55

Changing splits 56

Transactions – an overview

The following points are central to the way Money works:

- Money defines a transaction as anything which affects the balance of an account

- you enter transactions directly into the Register, a special window which lets you access the account, or via a form which simulates your chequebook

- within the account, transactions are entered into *fields*. The main fields are:

    - Num

    - Date

    - Payee

    - Payment

    - Deposit

    - Balance

These are contained within the Register (see page 39). Additional fields are also present in the Register form:

    - Pay to or From

    - Category/Sub-category

    - Memo

REMEMBER
Two further fields will also be present if you've allocated one or two classifications. See pages 48-52.

Transaction types

Transactions fall into various types:

- Cheque

- Deposit

- Transfer

- Withdrawal

- Cash Machine

Entering transactions (1)

Entering data into accounts using the Register is easy.
Carry out the following steps to create a new transaction:

Fields

REMEMBER

Re step 1 – this creates a new transaction. If you want to amend an existing one, highlight it and click the Edit button. Now carry out steps 3-4.

View bar

Click here

HANDY TIP

If the Register form isn't currently visible, click:

in the top left-hand corner of the Register's view bar. In the menu, click Transaction Forms.

2 Click a transaction tab

| Cheque | Deposit | Transfer | Withdrawal | Cash Machine |

New   Edit   Enter   Cancel   Number:
Date: 24/01/97
Pay to: Amount:
Category: Split
Memo:

REMEMBER

Re step 3 – for more information on how to enter data into the Register form, see later topics.

4 Click here to record the transaction

3 Type in the relevant data

Entering transactions (2)

You can also enter data *directly* into the Account Register.

Click the triangle in the Account Register view bar (see the Handy Tip on page 39 for how to do this). Now carry out the following steps:

(see the Handy Tip on page 39 for how to do this)

BEWARE **You can only use this method to enter data into certain fields. For example, you can't use it to apply categories or classifications...**

- By Date
  By Number
  By Entry Order
- All Transactions
  Unreconciled Transactions
- Top Line Only
  All Transaction Details   Ctrl+T
✔ Transaction Forms

| Deselect this

2 Click in the next empty line

Num	Date	Payee	C	Payment	Deposit	Balance
	12/11/96	(from Daren's account)		13.00		0.00
	27/01/97					

Ending Balance: £0.00

HANDY TIP **Re step 3 – press Enter when you've finished entering transaction data.**

3 Type in transaction details

Entering transactions (3)

Money provides various shortcuts which make entering transaction information even easier and more convenient.

AutoComplete

When you begin to type in text in a Register field, AutoComplete anticipates what you're about to type and – as soon as it recognises it – inserts the remaining text:

REMEMBER

If you no longer want to use AutoComplete, pull down the Tools menu and click Options. Activate the Editing tab. Deselect Use AutoComplete. Click OK.

Num	Date	Payee	C	Payment	Deposit	Balance
	12/11/96	(from Daren's account)		13.00		0.00
	27/01/97	auto Insurance Ltd				

Here, typing 'au' in the Payee field has produced one possible match…

Ending Balance: £0.00

Press Enter when the correct details are on-screen.

Even more usefully, entering a previously used **payee** prompts Money to insert *all* the information from the last transaction involving the payee:

HANDY TIP

If you need to change the data inserted by AutoComplete, just type over it in the normal way.

Num	Date	Payee	C	Payment	Deposit	Balance
	12/11/96	(from Daren's account)		13.00		0.00
	27/01/97	Gordons Garages		17.00		-17.00
	27/01/97					

Here, typing 'go' and then pressing Enter has inserted one entire transaction

Ending Balance: -£17.00

Entering transactions (4)

Pull-down calendars

When you type in text in the Date field, you can use the boxed arrow to the right:

You can also advance or recede dates by pressing the [+] or [-] keys respectively in the Numerical keypad on the right of the keyboard (irrespective of whether the Num Lock key has been activated).

Date: |27/01/97| ▾

Clicking the arrow produces an in-built calendar. Do the following:

Optional – click here to move back one month

	JAN 1997	
S M T W T F S
29 30 31 1 2 3 4
5 6 7 8 9 10 11
12 13 14 15 16 17 18
19 20 21 22 23 24 25
26 **27** 28 29 30 31 1
2 3 4 5 6 7 8

2 Optional – click here to move forward one month

3 Click a day to insert it into the Date field

Pull-down calculators

When you type in numbers in fields which relate to amounts, you can use the boxed arrow to the right. Click this to produce an in-built calculator:

7	8	9	/
4	5	6	*
1	2	3	-
0	.	±	+
C	←	=	

Use the calculator in the normal way. As you do so, the numbers you work with appear in the relevant Money field.

Moving between transactions

To enter data into a field, you can simply click in it and begin typing. If a field isn't visible, you can use the scroll bars to rectify this – a standard Windows technique. However, you can also use keyboard routes to find the appropriate field. This is sometimes the most convenient method.

The simplest method is to use the cursor keys (unaided) to move through accounts. This is often sufficient, but there are also shortcuts:

HANDY TIP

You can also use a specific dialog to move to particular transactions.

Press Ctrl+F. In the dialog, ensure the Text tab is active. Type in the text you want to find:

Type in text here

If you want to limit the search in other ways, click any of the other tabs and impose the relevant restrictions. Click Find to locate the specified transaction(s).

To go to a transaction, right-click over its entry in the (extended) dialog; in the menu, click the relevant Go To... entry.

If the search was abortive, click the Close button to close the dialog.

Tab	moves the insertion point to the next field (and – in the process – records any additions or alterations you've made)
Shift+Tab	moves the insertion point to the previous field (and – in the process – records any additions or alterations you've made)
Ctrl+↑	moves to the previous transaction in an account
Ctrl+↓	moves to the next transaction in an account
Ctrl+Home	moves to the first transaction in an account
Ctrl+End	moves to the last transaction in an account
Page Up	moves one screen upward through transactions
Page Down	moves one screen down through transactions

Categories – an overview

Traditional book-based accounts make use of identifying headings – for instance, outgoings are entered as 'Stationery' or 'Drawings'. Money takes this practice and extends it almost infinitely, and with much more detail. It does this by allowing you to assign 'categories' to transactions.

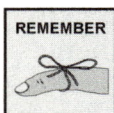

REMEMBER

Categories fall into two main divisions: Income (applied to deposits) or Expense (applied to withdrawals).

Categories are convenient labels; you can – and should – use them to:

* organise your accounts and make them much more detailed

* produce tailor-made reports – see Section 7 for more information

* produce customised graphs – see Section 7 for more information

Limiting reports or graphs to specific categories produces a much more precise result.

Sub-categories

To ensure even greater precision, categories can be – and very often are – divided into sub-categories. For example, the Expense category 'Pet Care' is split into:

HANDY TIP

Money comes with a sizeable number of categories and sub-categories. However, you can easily create your own. See the 'Creating categories' topics later.

* Food

* Supplies

* Veterinarian

Differentiation

Money differentiates between categories and sub-categories by placing them in separate fields:

| Pet Care ▾ | Food ▾ |

Category and Sub-category fields in the Register form

Using categories/sub-categories

The use of categories and sub-categories makes for great precision. However, you need to exercise some care in how you apply them.

For example, if you're entering a payment to your regional water company into your account, you'll probably apply the following preset combination:

Category: Bills

Sub-category: Water & Sewer

By doing this, you ensure that there is no possible doubt as to the identity of the withdrawal. However, when you come to have Money compile a report, you probably won't need this. It will probably be sufficient merely to have the report based on *all* 'Bills' payments...

Applying categories and sub-categories

Within the relevant Register form, do the following:

You can only apply categories and sub-categories from within the Register form; you can't impose them directly into accounts.

Carry out steps 1-3 when you enter a new transaction, or amend an existing one.

3 Click here

Num	Date	Payee	C	Payment	Deposit	Balance
	16/01/97	Mr Booth			897.00	1,044.00
	16/01/97	(Tax set aside)		224.00		820.00
	22/01/97	(cash point withdrawl)		10.00		810.00
	31/01/97	{Tax Authority}		24.00		786.00
	31/01/97	(Transfer)		75.00		711.00
EEpay	31/01/97	Credit Ltd		178.00		533.00
	04/02/97	Cash		25.00		508.00
	21/02/97	Cash		15.00		493.00
	27/02/97	Simmons Constructors			850.00	1,343.00
	27/02/97	(Tax set aside)		381.00		962.00
	28/02/97	{Tax Authority}		24.00		938.00
	28/02/97	(Transfer)		75.00		863.00

Ending Balance: £863.00

View: All Transactions, by Date

Cheque | **Deposit** | Transfer | Withdrawal | Cash Machine

New   Edit   Enter   Cancel

Number:
Date: 27/02/97

From: Simmons Constructors   Amount: 850.00

Category: Income - John   Gross Income   Split

Memo:

1 Click here; select a category in the list

2 Click here; select a sub-category in the list

Creating categories

When you allocate categories and/or sub-categories to your transactions, you can select from numerous ready-made choices which cover most conceivable situations. In the early stages of your use of Money, this will certainly be sufficient. As your experience increases, however, you'll probably want to create your own. Creating categories and sub-categories is easy and convenient, and even fun.

Creating a new category

In the course of entering a new transaction or amending an existing one, do the following:

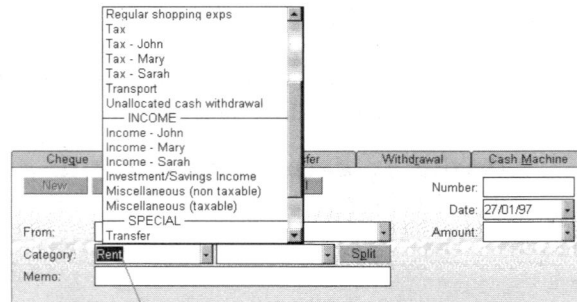

| Regular shopping exps |
| Tax |
| Tax - John |
| Tax - Mary |
| Tax - Sarah |
| Transport |
| Unallocated cash withdrawal |
| —— INCOME —— |
| Income - John |
| Income - Mary |
| Income - Sarah |
| Investment/Savings Income |
| Miscellaneous (non taxable) |
| Miscellaneous (taxable) |
| —— SPECIAL —— |
| Transfer |

Cheque   fer   Withdrawal   Cash Machine

New   Number:

Date: 27/01/97

From:

Amount:

Category: Rent   Split

Memo:

Click in the Category field and type in a name for the new category

Press Enter. Now do the following:

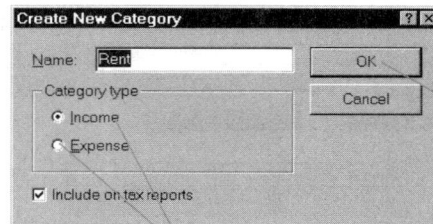

Create New Category ? ✕

Name: Rent   OK

Category type   Cancel

⊙ Income

○ Expense

☑ Include on tax reports

3 Click here

2 Click a category type

Creating sub-categories

Creating a new sub-category is a slightly different process to creating a category, because it isn't necessary to allocate a type.

Creating a new sub-category

In the course of entering a new transaction or amending an existing one, and after carrying out ONE of the following:

- selecting an existing category

- creating a new category

do the following:

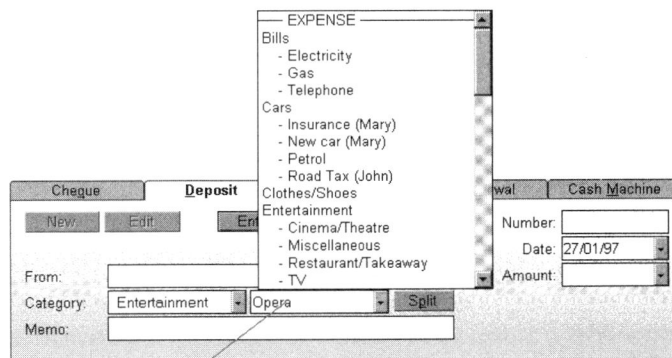

Click here and type in a name
for the new sub-category

HANDY TIP

If you change your mind and want to allocate the new sub-category to a different category, click here:
In the list, click a category. Finally, carry out step 2.

Press Enter. Now do the following:

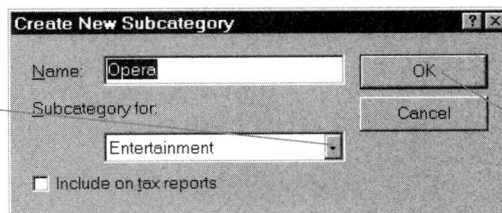

2 Click here

Classifications – an overview

Money has another feature you can use to make your transactions even more precise: classifications.

It's important to be clear in your mind as to the distinction between classifications and categories. Categories make it very easy to catalogue transactions, but they can sometimes be restrictive. Take the case of a small business proprietor working from home. He'll clearly have to pay both domestic and commercial telephone charges, but there will be a need to distinguish between the two. Money has the following preset category/sub-category:

Category:	Bills
Sub-category:	Telephone

but this doesn't make the necessary distinction. Of course, it would be possible to create a new category/sub-category combination e.g.:

Category:	Bills
Sub-category	Work telephone

but this is a less than elegant solution (though a practicable one). It is better and more convenient to create a new Classification.

Classifications are 'types'. They offer as much precision as categories, and can be further divided into:

items	instances of a classification. For example, in the case of the existing classification 'Properties' (see the Remember tip), each building would be one item.
sub-items	a way to subdivide items. To continue the above example, if each building consisted of more than one flat, each flat would be a sub-item.

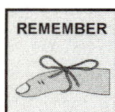

REMEMBER

Money comes with several pre-defined classifications:
Family members
Properties
Projects
Hobbies
Holidays
Job expenses
However, they aren't active until you create them. (See pages 50-51.)

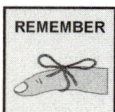

REMEMBER

Each Money file can have a maximum of 2 active classifications.

Using classifications

Using classification items and sub-items to catalogue your transactions is easy. However, you should bear the following in mind:

- in the early days of your use of Money, you probably won't need to use items and sub-items. However, they will be invaluable later

- items/sub-items *complement* (but don't replace) the use of categories/sub-categories

BEWARE **To carry out the procedures listed here, you must first have created one or two classifications – see pages 50-51.**

Applying a classification item

Within the Register form, do the following:

2 Click here

| Cheque | Deposit | Transfer | Withdrawal | Cash Machine |

New	Edit	Enter	Cancel	Number: 361
				Date: 28/01/97
Pay to:				Amount:
Category:			Split	
Properties:				
Memo:	112 Upper Moulton Ave. Plimpton			

Click here; select an item in the list

REMEMBER **When you've created one or two classifications, Money inserts extra fields in the Register form:**

Applying a classification sub-item

Within the Register form, do the following:

2 Click here

| Cheque | Deposit | Transfer | Withdrawal | Cash Machine |

New	Edit	Enter	Cancel	Number: 361
				Date: 28/01/97
Pay to:				Amount:
Category:			Split	
Properties:				
Memo:		112 Upper Moulton Ave. Plimpton - Flat A		

Click here; select a subitem in the list

Creating classifications (1)

In the Contents area, do the following:

HANDY TIP

Although you can apply items and sub-items from within the Account Register, you can only create them within the Payees and Categories area.

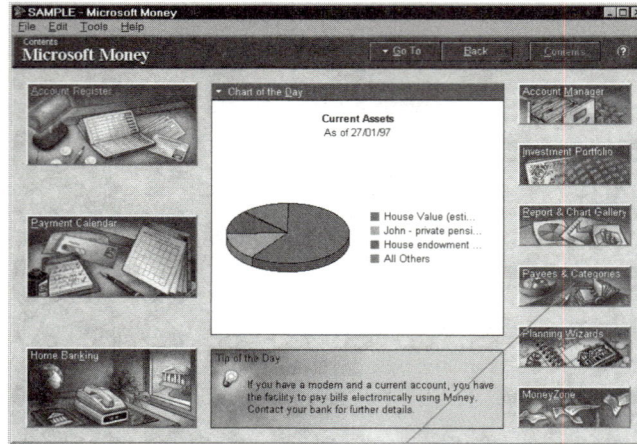

Click here

Now carry out the following steps:

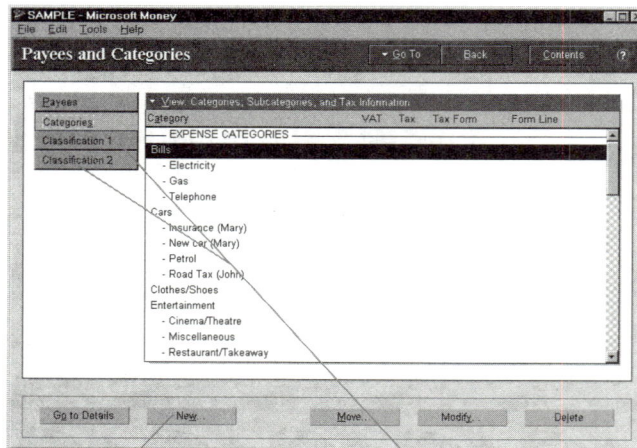

5 Click here

2 Click one of these

Creating classifications (2)

HANDY TIP — **Steps 5-7 add an item to the overall classification. If you want to add a sub-item to the item, click it in the Payees and Categories area:**

Item

Now follow step 5 on page 50. In the dialog which appears, do the following:

Click here

In the Name field, type in sub-item details. Finally, click OK.

4 Click here

3 Click a classification, or type in your own

Carry out step 5 on page 50. Do the following:

6 Type in item details

7 Click here

The newly created classification and item

Changing categories/classifications

HANDY TIP

To amend a sub-category, click it in step 2. Follow step 3. Complete the dialog which launches, then click OK.

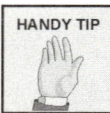

It's sometimes necessary to undertake category and classification housekeeping. You can:

• rename a category/classification

• delete a category/classification

• (in the case of categories) apply a different type

Revising a category

Follow step 1 on page 50. Carry out the following:

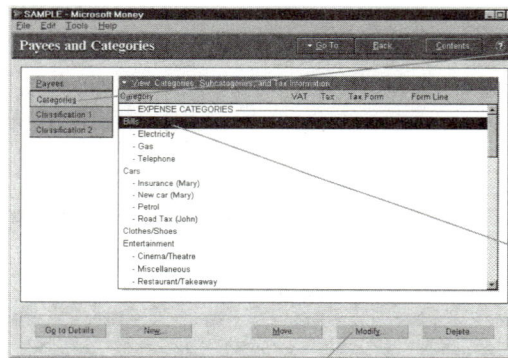

HANDY TIP

To amend an item or sub-item, click either of the Classification buttons:

| Properties |
| Classification 2 |

in step 1. In step 2, select an item or sub-item. Follow step 3. Complete the dialog which launches, then click OK.

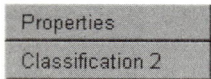

1 Click here

2 Click a category

3 Click here

Now carry out step 4 below to rename the category and/or step 5 to apply a new category type. Finally, carry out step 6:

HANDY TIP

To delete a category, sub-category, item or sub-item, click it in step 2. Then click the Delete button. If a message launches, click OK to proceed with the deletion.

4 Type in a new name

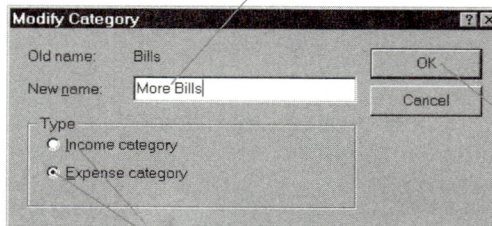

6 Click here

5 Click a new category type

Splits – an overview

So far, we've seen how categories and classifications can be applied to transactions. This is more than sufficient for the majority of transactions, but consider the following situation.

A householder receives two premium requests from the same insurance company, at more or less the same time. Clearly, though, he won't want to write *two* separate cheques. Instead, he'll write one for the full amount, and this will appear in his Money account as a single transaction. However, it would help his accounts considerably if he could differentiate between the two amounts, since they are functionally distinct. In fact, he really has to do this to avoid the possibility of confusion in the future.

This sort of situation requires a special approach. Additional examples of situations which need this are:

- salary cheques, which can profitably be itemised to show the individual components

- self-employed writers receiving cheques which relate to multiple commissions

- transactions which relate to multiple payees

Transaction splits

How does Money solve this problem? By allowing transactions to be 'split'. This is simply the process of applying multiple categories (and even classifications) to a single transaction. In general terms, and continuing our original example, you could split the joint insurance payment by creating two new category/sub-category combinations:

Insurance/Home

Insurance/Car

to the overall amount. Each combination would have its share of the total premium allocated to it.

REMEMBER

Money comes with a preset category called 'Household expenses'; one of the associated sub-categories is 'Insurance (building & content)'

Clearly, these are inadequate for our purpose here. For how to create your own category/sub-category combinations, see pages 46-47 and 50-51.

Creating splits

To apply a split, carry out the following steps (in the course of entering the appropriate transaction):

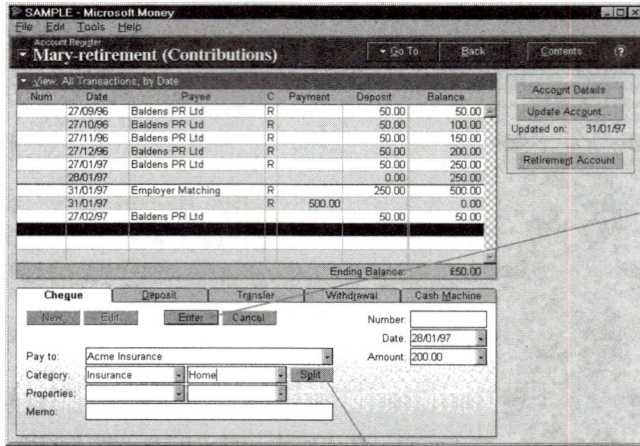

5 Click here

Click here

HANDY TIP

Repeat steps 2 and 3 for as many components as you want to include in the split. Carry out step 4 when you've finished creating it.

HANDY TIP

If you want, you can also impose a classification (if you've created one).
To apply an item and subitem, do the following:

| Insurance | Car |

Click here; choose an item

Click here; choose a subitem

Finally, follow step 4.

2 Apply or create the relevant category/sub-category

3 Type in the amount for the split component

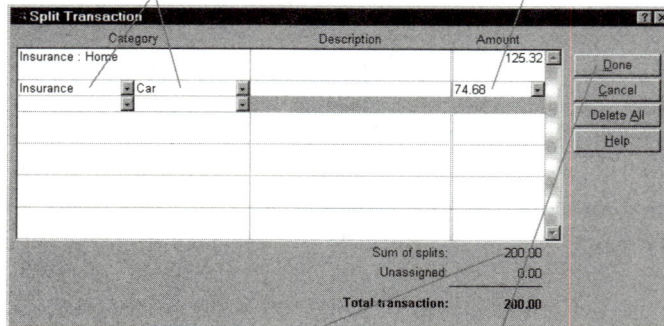

This balance is updated as you enter the split

4 Click here

Revising splits – an overview

Revising splits which have already been set up – a task which is sometimes necessary – is a fairly straightforward job, but there are certain points you need to bear in mind:

After you've entered a figure in the Amount field in the Split Transaction dialog...

Amount
125.32
64.68

First split

Remainder in next line

In this example, the Register transaction total would be £190 (125.32+64.68).

...Money subtracts this from the Register transaction total and inserts the remainder in the next free line.

So far, so good. If you alter any of the splits, Money updates the Register with the revised total when you confirm the change. However, if you alter the Register transaction total directly, *without altering the splits*, Money – unsurprisingly – registers a discrepancy. You need to tell it how to resolve it. You can do this by carrying out ONE of the following:

- revising the transaction total back to the earlier, correct version

- amending one or more splits, or inserting one or more new splits (the net value of the alterations being equal to the amount of the shortfall)

The ideal

You know that you've successfully balanced a transaction and its splits when the Unassigned field shows '0.00'.

Sum of splits:	200.00
Unassigned:	0.00
Total transaction:	**200.00**

The sign of a correct split

Changing splits

From within the relevant transaction, carry out the following steps when you've entered a new transaction total which doesn't match the total within the Split Transaction dialog:

Original splits total

New total

Click here

2 Click here

Now carry out step 3 OR 4 below. Finally, carry out step 5:

REMEMBER
After step 5, carry out step 1 again to record your amendments.

3 Adjust one or more existing splits

5 Click here

4 Add one or more new splits

Accounts

Use this chapter to learn about the Account Manager. You'll create new accounts and open/amend existing ones. You'll also discover how to switch between accounts, and how to close (hide) accounts which are no longer current. Then you'll transfer money from one account to another, and delete/void specific transactions. Finally, you'll print out your account, category, classification or payee details.

Covers

Accounts – an overview 58

The Account Manager 59

Creating a new account 60

Opening accounts 63

Account editing – an overview 64

Editing account details 65

Closing accounts 66

Deleting accounts 67

Transaction transfers – an overview 68

Transferring money 69

Deleting & voiding – an overview 70

Deleting & voiding in action 71

Print options 72

Accounts – an overview

In Section 3, we looked at how to enter transactions into the account which was set up as part of the file created when Money was installed.

Many users find they only need this one account; others, on the other hand, discover that as they become more proficient with Money there is a need to create further accounts within the default file. A common example would be the user who needs to utilise Money to manage his domestic affairs and a small business. In this situation, having separate accounts for both makes a lot of sense. You don't *need* to do this – after all, you can use categories and/or classifications to differentiate perfectly adequately between transaction types – but it is both logical and convenient.

Money makes creating further accounts easy.

Other reasons for creating new accounts are:

- to handle individual businesses separately

- to handle petty cash transactions separately

- to track shares

- to track liabilities

- to track credit card debts

- to track loans

- to track retirement plans

The last six examples involve Money account types which are beyond the scope of this book. However, the procedures for creating them are fundamentally identical with the standard account type.

Money provides a convenient base from which to work with accounts: the Account Manager.

The Account Manager

The Account Manager is a highly convenient and useful central focus for work with Money accounts. You can use it to:

- create new accounts

- open accounts

- modify accounts

- mark accounts as Favourites

- delete accounts

- close accounts

- view a balance summary for all your accounts

- view all individual account balances

Launching the Account Manager

In the Contents area, do the following:

Click here

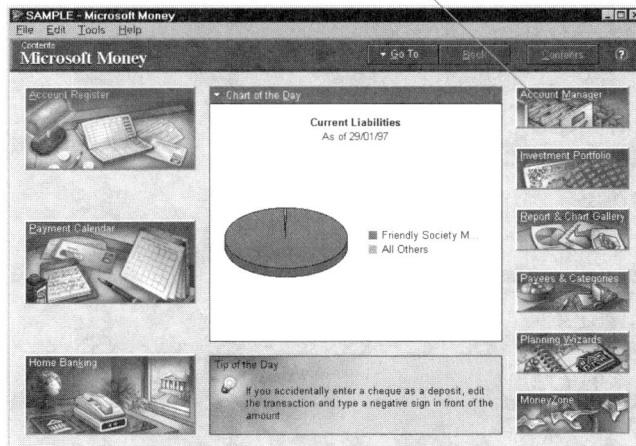

Creating a new account (1)

BEWARE

If you've created further Money files (see Section 2), make sure you've opened the correct one *before* you start to create a new account.

Money provides a special Wizard to help you create new accounts. The New Account Wizard leads you by the hand through the process of account creation, asking all the questions which need to be answered.

Using the New Account Wizard

Ensure you have your chequebook or Building Society passbook to hand. Then launch the Account Manager – see page 59 for how to do this. Carry out the following steps:

REMEMBER

Here: the Account Manager displays the total balance for *all* accounts within the current file.

If you want to see the *individual* balances, however, click:

▼

in the View bar. In the menu, click Account Balances.

View bar

Click here

Now complete the various Wizard dialogs which appear:

HANDY TIP

Re step 2 – if no financial institution is involved with the account you're creating, leave this field blank.

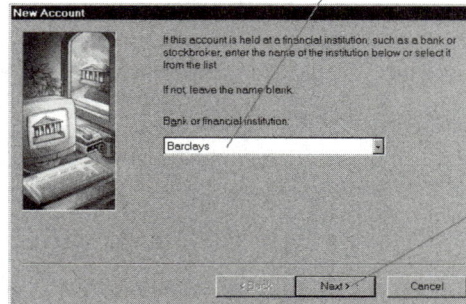

2 Type in the Bank or Building Society name

3 Click here

Creating a new account (2)

Now carry out the following additional steps:

1 Select an account type

Re step 1 –
since we're
concerned
here with
HANDY TIP
the most commonly
used Money
account, click
Current.

New Account at Barclays

What kind of account would you like to set up at Barclays?

Asset
Bank
Cash
Credit Card
Current
Investment
Liability
Line of Credit
Loan
Other
Retirement
Savings

Use Current Accounts to track all your day to day financial activity, including debit card transactions.

2 Click here

< Back   Next >   Cancel

3 Name the account

New Account at Barclays

What do you want to call this Current account at Barclays?

Barclays Current

4 Click here

< Back   Next >   Cancel

Step 5 is
optional: it
isn't
REMEMBER
essential
to enter the account
number into your
Money account, but
it can be useful to
have it there...

5 Type in the account number

New Account at Barclays

What is the account number?

If you don't know the account number, just leave it blank. You can always enter it later in Account Details. The account number is not required for you to use Money, but sometimes it's convenient to have in your Money file.

6 Click here

< Back   Next >   Cancel

Creating a new account (3)

Carry out the following additional steps:

REMEMBER **Re step 1 – enter the balance from your latest statement.**
If there are outstanding transactions which haven't hit the statement yet, don't worry: Money's reconciliation process (see Section 6) will pick these up later.

1 Enter the account balance

New Account at Barclays

What's the balance of this account?

`1,000.00`

What is the currency for this account?

`Default Currency £`

Enter the ending balance from your last statement. If you want to start your record keeping from an earlier date, enter the ending balance from the earlier statement, and then enter all transactions from that statement until now.

Note: If you want to track this account from the day you opened it, enter zero. If you don't know your current balance, enter an estimate. You can change it later before you balance the account.

`< Back`   `Next >`   `Cancel`

2 Click here

3 Click here

New Account at Barclays

If you have other accounts at this bank, you can also set them up now.

○ I have other accounts at this bank.

◉ I have no other accounts at this bank.
   Choose this if you have no other accounts to set up, or if you have others but they're with a different bank.

`< Back`   `Next >`   `Cancel`

4 Click here

5 Click here

New Account at Barclays

Would you like to find out what Online Services are available with this bank?

○ Yes, I want to find out about the Online Services.

◉ No, not now.

`< Back`   `Finish`   `Cancel`

6 Click here

Opening accounts

After you've created an additional account, you need to open it in order to work with it. You can do this:

- from within the Account Manager

- from within the Account Register

Handy Tip: You can change the way the Account Manager displays accounts. You can vary the size of account icons (there are 2 options: Large or Small). Or you can display accounts as a list.

Position the cursor anywhere in the Account Manager display area (but not over an account entry). Right-click and do the following:

Click one of these

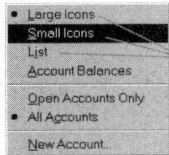

Opening an account from the Account Manager

Launch the Account Manager – see page 59 for how to do this. Carry out the following:

Display area

Double-click an account icon

Opening an account from the Account Register

In the Account Register, carry out the following steps:

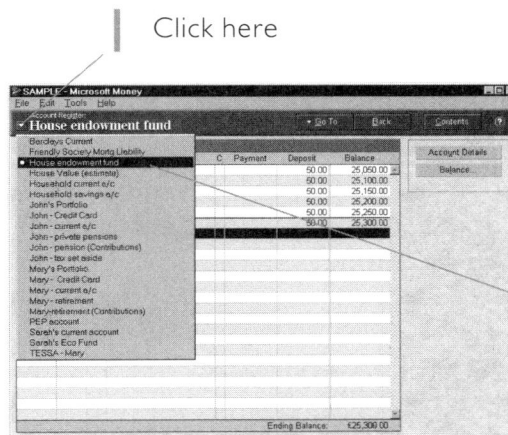

Click here

2 Click an account

Account editing – an overview

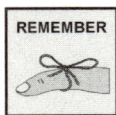

So far, we've looked at how to use the Account Manager to:

- create new accounts

- open existing accounts

However, you can also use it to:

- amend account *details,* basic descriptive information relating to the way the account functions. Features you can change include (according to the type of account):

  - the account name

  - the currency used

  - contact details relating to the person you deal with

  - whether the account is VAT enabled

  - the account number

  - the opening balance

- mark accounts as Favourites (as many as nine)

- close ('hide') inactive accounts

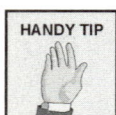

- delete accounts

Remember that the process of deleting accounts is irreversible. The following actions happen when you proceed with a deletion:

- all recorded transactions which relate to the deleted account are expunged form the host file and lost forever

- all information relating to the account is destroyed

Click here

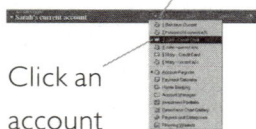

Click an account

Because account deletions are permanent, Money launches a warning message before complying with your instruction. To proceed with the deletion, you have to type in 'yes' and click the appropriate button.

Editing account details

REMEMBER

You can also launch the Account Details screen from within the Account Register. Do the following:

Click here

> Account Details
>
> Balance...

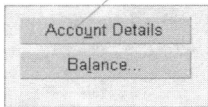

Within the Account Manager, do the following:

1 Click an account

HANDY TIP

To rename an account or apply a new type to it, click here: Complete the Modify Account dialog as appropriate, then click OK.

2 Click here

3 Complete any of these fields

HANDY TIP

The panel on the right of the Accounts Details screen provides a visual statement of how the selected account stands. In the case of Current accounts, Money charts the running balance.

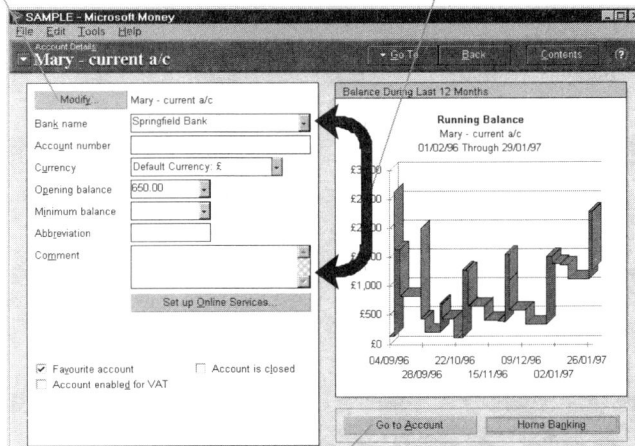

4 Click here

Closing accounts

Money lets you 'close' accounts. Accounts which are closed no longer appear in account lists (for instance, the menu of available accounts which launches when you click:

in the Account Register Navigation Bar).

Hiding accounts is useful when both of the following conditions are met:

REMEMBER

A more drastic alternative to closing accounts is deleting them – see page 67.

- the accounts concerned are little used (probably because they refer to expired periods)

- you want to retain the transactions in the accounts, so that any reports and charts you generate take them into account

Closing an account

Within the Account Manager, do the following:

Right-click an account

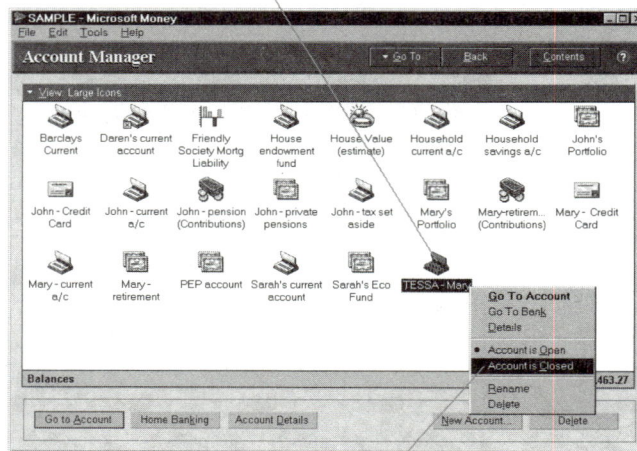

2 Click here

Deleting accounts

Money lets you delete accounts. When you delete an account, all the transactions associated with it are permanently and   irreversibly removed.

HANDY TIP

It's a good idea to make a backup copy of the host file before you delete one of its accounts. For how to do this, see page 27.

Removing an account

Within the Account Manager, do the following:

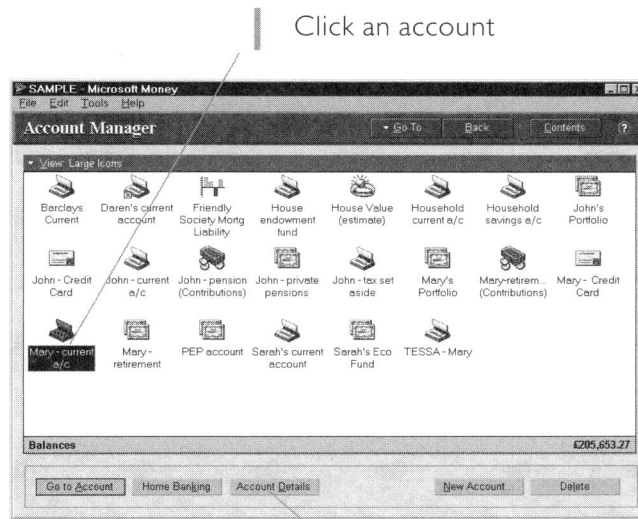

Click an account

2 Click here

BEWARE

Be very sure you want to proceed with the deletion before you carry out step 3.

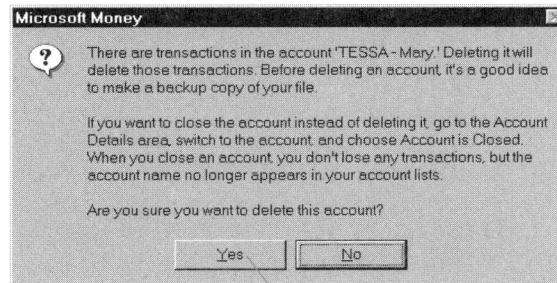

Microsoft Money

There are transactions in the account 'TESSA - Mary.' Deleting it will delete those transactions. Before deleting an account, it's a good idea to make a backup copy of your file.

If you want to close the account instead of deleting it, go to the Account Details area, switch to the account, and choose Account is Closed. When you close an account, you don't lose any transactions, but the account name no longer appears in your account lists.

Are you sure you want to delete this account?

Yes   No

3 Click here

Transaction transfers – an overview

There are situations when it becomes very useful to be able to transfer money from one Money account to another. Examples are:

- transferring money from a Building Society account to a Bank account (or vice versa)

- transferring money from a Bank account to a Credit Card account

Money makes this process very easy and straightforward. It does this by not making you enter transfers twice

This may require explanation.

Let's suppose that you want to transfer money from a Building Society account into your current Bank account. Clearly, there are two inherent transactions here: the withdrawal out of your Building Society account, and the consequent deposit in your Bank account. Rather than have you insert both, Money lets you simply enter one in *either* account. When you enter it, you cross-refer it to the other account. As long as you enter the details correctly (the entire process is very easy and straightforward), Money ties everything up automatically.

When you enter a transfer, you can combine it with a classification (but not a category). For instance, if you're transferring money out of a Building Society account to pay the telephone bill, you might catalogue it as:

Overall classification: Transfers

Classification item: Abbey National

Classification sub-item: Telephone

These, of course, are merely suggestions...

Transferring money

To transfer money from one account to another, do the following in the Account Register:

Click here

3 Click here

2 Click here; in the list, select the recipient account. Then complete the remaining form fields, as appropriate

The recipient account, with the transferred transaction highlighted

Deleting & voiding – an overview

Sometimes it's necessary to delete or void transactions. However, it's important to be clear about the difference.

Deletion

Deleting a transaction erases it completely and permanently. Probably the only valid reason for deleting a transaction is if you've entered it into the wrong account.

Voiding

Voiding a transaction leaves it intact within the Account Register. However, its transaction amount is not included in the account balance.

Voiding is considerably more useful than deletion. The classic situation where voiding is advisable is an incorrect cheque. It's necessary to stop it, clearly, but at the same time there is a need to retain an entry in the Register for future reference.

See the illustration below for an example of a voided transaction:

REMEMBER

When a transaction is voided, Money inserts **VOID** in the Balance field and R in the C (i.e. Cleared) field:

Num	Date	Payee	C	Payment	Deposit	Balance
	26/12/96	Cash		15.00		467.00
	31/12/96	{Tax Authority}		24.00		443.00
	31/12/96	(Transfer)		75.00		368.00
EEpay	31/12/96	Credit Ltd		180.00		188.00
	02/01/97	Cash		10.00		178.00
364	02/01/97	Roger Hilton		31.00		147.00
	16/01/97	Mr. Booth			897.00	
	16/01/97	(Tax set-aside)		24.00		810.00
	22/01/97	(cash point withdr		.00		
	27/01/97				0.6	
	30/01/97	John Smith	R		35.0	**VOID**
	31/01/97	{Tax Authority}		0		786.00

Account Details

Balance...

Ending Balance

| Cheque | Deposit | | Withdrawal | Ca |

New | Edit | Enter | Cancel

To: John - current a/c   Date: 30/01/97
From: Household current a/c   Amount: 35.00
Pay to: John Smith
Properties:
Memo: Return of loan   **VOID**

Deleting & voiding in action

Deleting a transaction

Within the Account Register, do the following:

Right-click a transaction

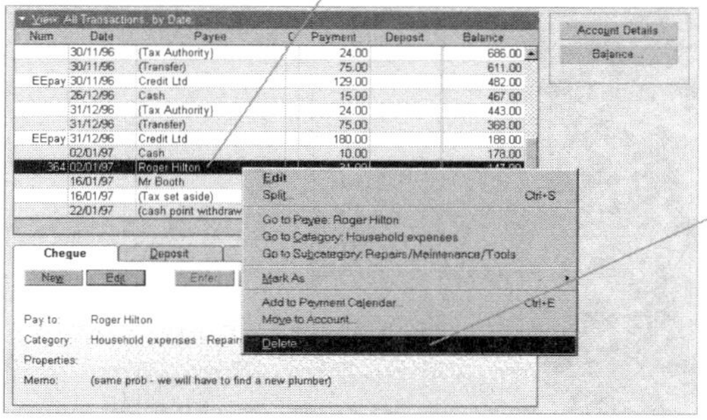

2 Click here

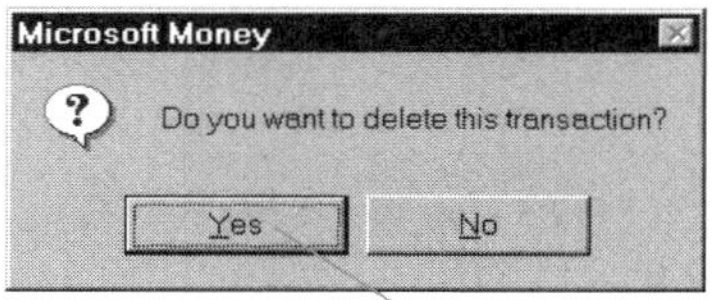

3 Click here

Voiding a transaction

Within the Account Register, do the following:

HANDY TIP

You can 'unvoid' a previously voided transaction by repeating steps 1-3. In the message which appears, do the following:

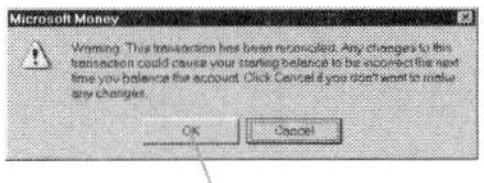

Click here

Right-click a transaction

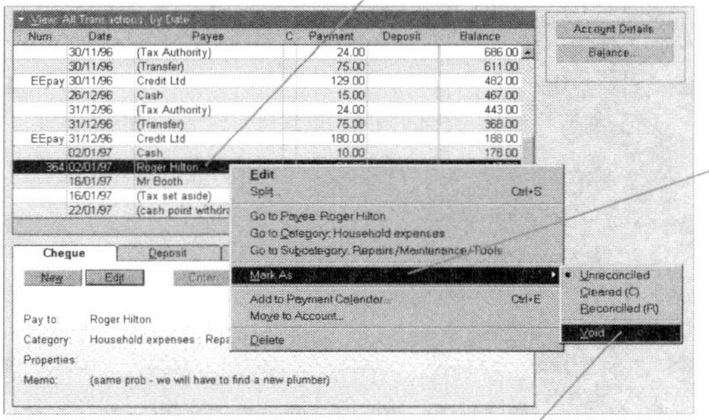

2 Click here

3 Click here

Print options

Before you start printing, ensure the correct printer is selected – for how to do this, see your Windows documentation.

Money lets you print out details of current transactions. You do this by printing the contents of the active account (but not the screen itself). You can also print category and classification lists. This is especially useful in the case of categories. When the number of categories you use is large, it can sometimes be preferable to refer to a printed list to find the one you want to use than to scroll through the on-screen Category drop-down list.

Printing the Account Register contents
Within the Register, press Ctrl+P. Do the following:

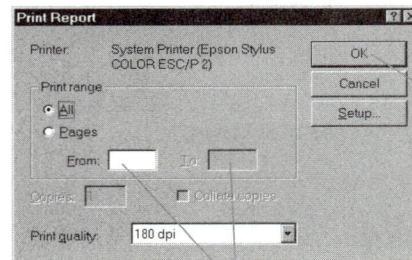

2 Click here to begin the print run

1 Enter start and end page numbers, if appropriate

You can also print out a list of payees. Simply click the Payees button: then follow steps 1 and 2 above.

Printing lists
From within the Payees and Categories area, do the following:

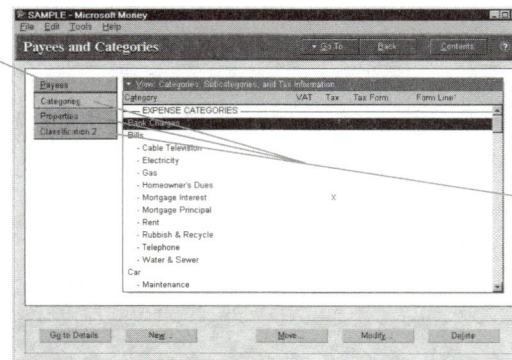

Click one of these

Now press Ctrl+P and follow steps 1 and 2 above.

Scheduling Transactions

Many of the transactions that you have to deal with involve a sum of money which changes hands at regular intervals. For example, standing orders withdraw a fixed amount from your bank account, and direct debits withdraw a variable amount, while pay cheques deposit a variable amount.

This section explains how to save time and effort by scheduling these frequently used transactions in the Payment Calendar, so that you only have to enter their details once. You'll use Money's reminder systems to ensure that you never miss a withdrawal/deposit instalment, and finally you'll enter pending transactions into the Account Register.

Covers

The Payment Calendar 74

Setting up recurring transactions 76

Amending scheduled entries 78

Dealing with reminders 80

Customising reminders 82

Entering scheduled transactions 83

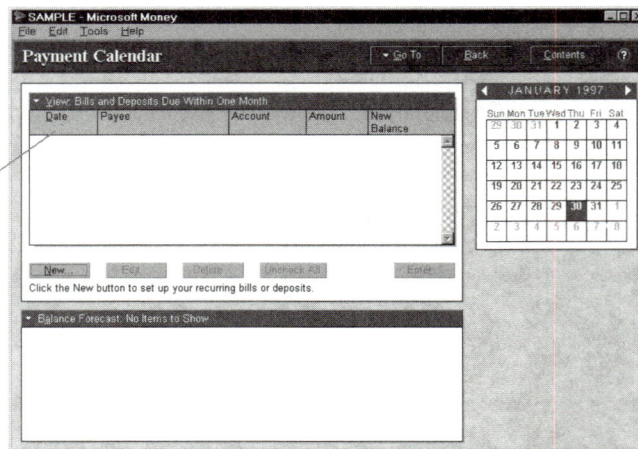

The Payment Calendar (1)

Use the Payment Calendar to enter standing orders and direct debits into your accounts. (See pages 83-84 for how to do so.)

Money provides a shortcut – the Payment Calendar – which saves you entering recurring transactions (i.e. those which have to be entered into the Account Register repetitively) more than once. You can use the Payment Calendar to automate:

*   bills

*   deposits (e.g. salary cheques)

*   transaction transfers

Eligible bills include:

You can also use the Payment Calendar to have Money remind you when a *one-off* payment is due. Use this technique for especially important transactions.
   (See pages 80-82 for how to work with reminders.)

–   rent payments

–   utility payments

–   loans

–   life insurance instalments

–   mortgages

–   council tax payments

–   insurance payments

This is the View section – scheduled transactions appear here.

The Payment Calendar

The Payment Calendar (2)

Broadly speaking, working with the Payment Calendar to automate the handling of recurring transactions is a three-stage process:

- entering the transaction(s) into the View section of the Payment Calendar

- responding when Money reminds you that one or more recurring transactions are due to be entered into the Account Register

- entering the approved transaction(s) into the Register (at this stage, you make sure your accounts contain enough funds to meet the highlighted transaction)

Launching the Payment Calendar

In the Contents area, do the following:

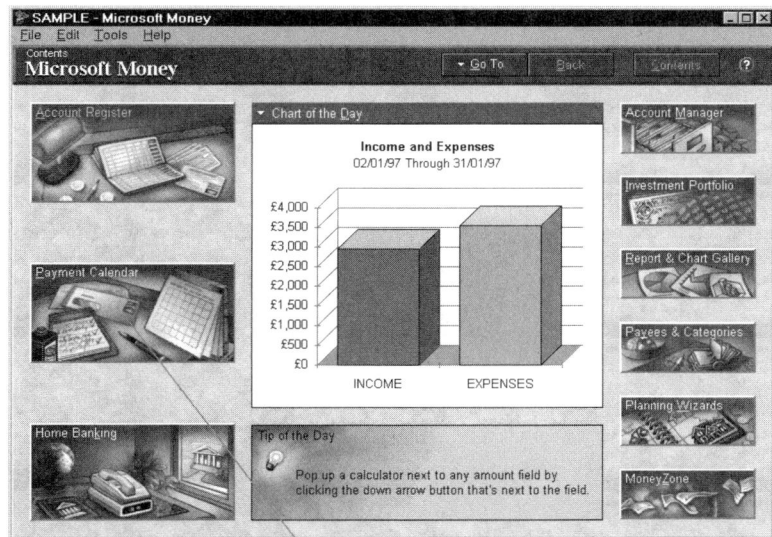

Click here

Setting up recurring transactions (1)

Open the account into which you want to insert the transaction. Launch the Payment Calendar – see page 75 for how to do this. Now do the following:

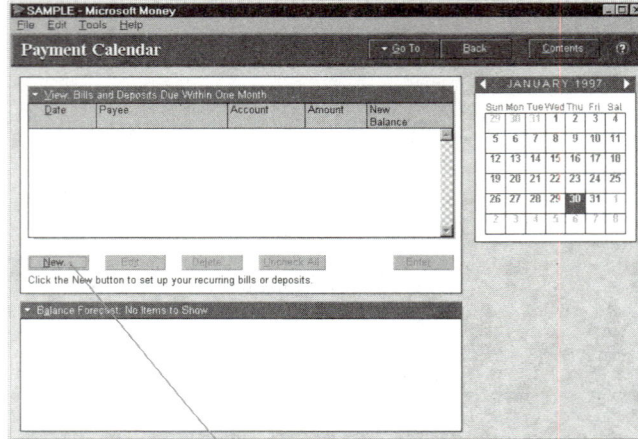

Click here

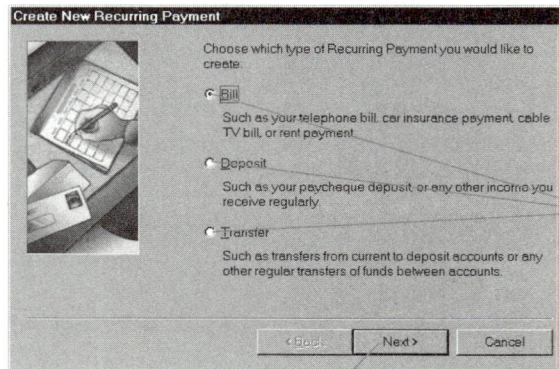

2 Click a transaction type

3 Click here

Setting up recurring transactions (2)

Now carry out the following steps:

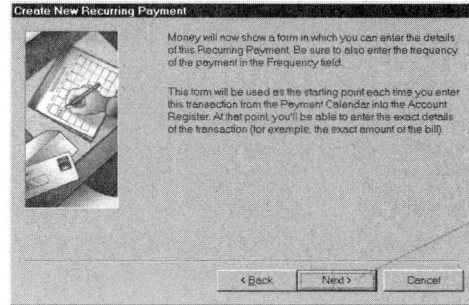

4 Click here

5 Click here; in the list, select
a payment frequency

**Money
provides a
handy
form to
help you enter the
necessary
information.**

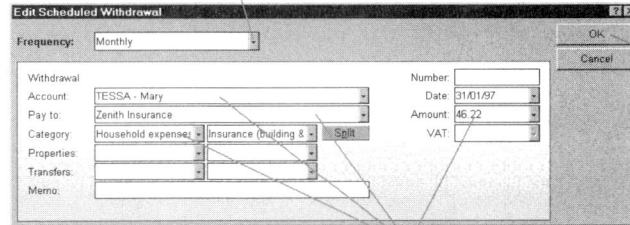

7 Click
here

6 Complete the relevant fields

The inserted transaction

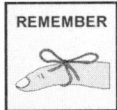

**The
envelope
icon
indicates
that one or more
reminders are due
on the given date:**

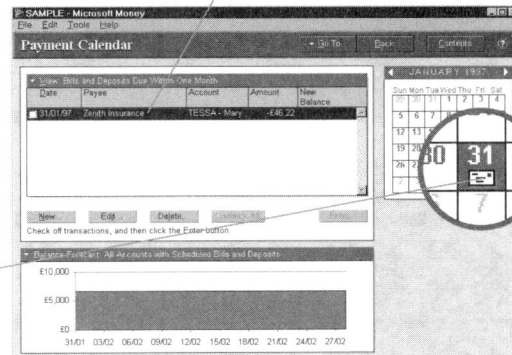

Amending scheduled entries (1)

You can revise the details for scheduled transactions, if you want.

This is especially useful if you need to:

- change the payment frequency

- change the payment amount

However, you can only revise the details for *all* instances of a given transaction. (If you only need to alter one specific instance, you can do so when you come to enter the transaction into the Register – see page 84.)

You can also delete scheduled entries. If you do this, you can opt to delete:

- all instances of the transaction

or

- merely the current instance

Revising scheduled transaction details
In the Payment Calendar, do the following:

Click a transaction

You can use the in-built calendar:
to view and select transactions associated with specific dates – see page 83.

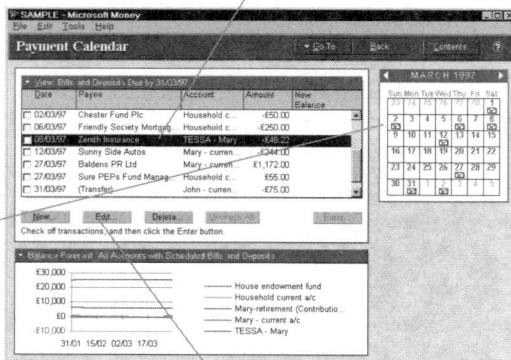

2 Click here

Amending scheduled entries (2)

Now carry out step 3 below to amend the payment frequency, and/or step 4 if you need to revise any of the other fields. Finally, carry out step 5:

3 Click here; in the list, select a payment frequency

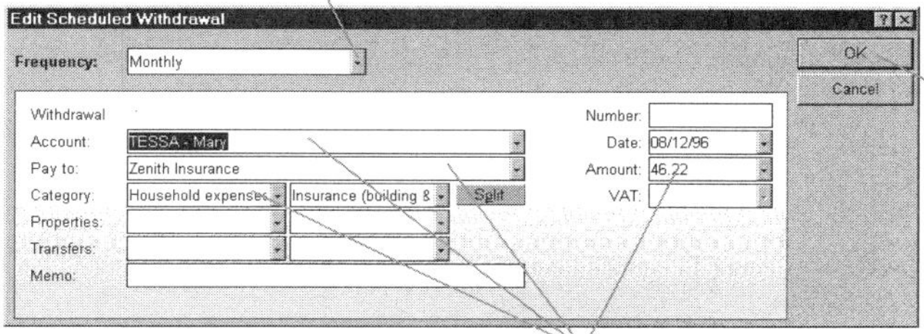

5 Click here

4 Amend the relevant fields

Deleting scheduled transactions

In the Payment Calendar, do the following:

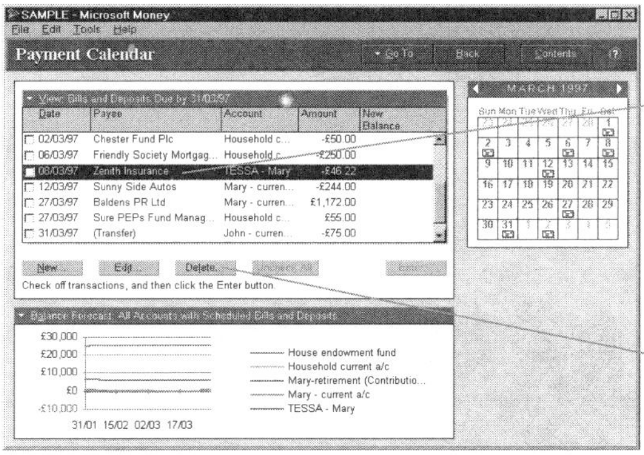

1 Click a transaction

2 Click here

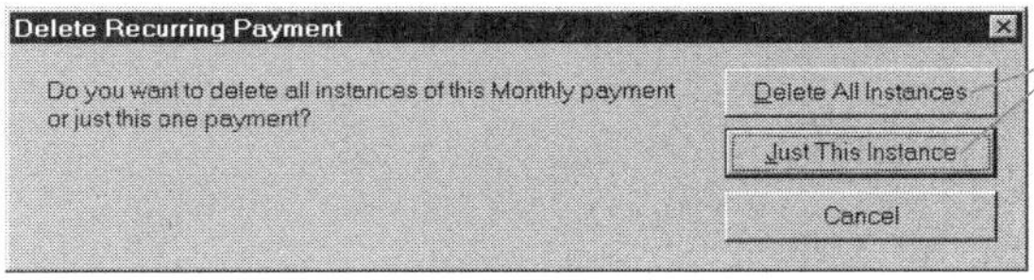

3 Click either of these

Dealing with reminders (1)

Money provides two reminder systems:

* the Payment Calendar itself

* a special icon on the Windows Task Bar

Using the Payment Calendar reminder

When one or more transactions are due, Money displays the following in the Contents screen:

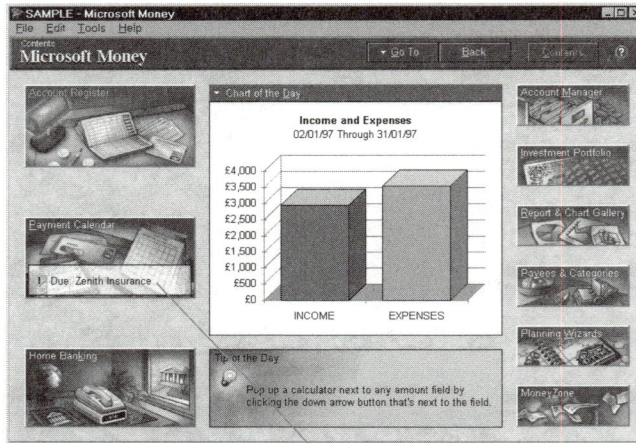

Transaction reminder

To activate the reminder, do the following:

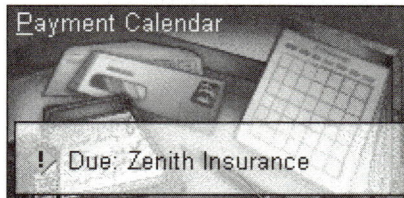

Click here

For what to do next, see pages 83-84.

Dealing with reminders (2)

Using the Task Bar reminder

When one or more transactions are due, Money displays the
following in the Windows Task Bar:

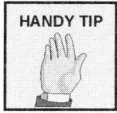

Money's reminder icon

HANDY TIP

**The Task
Bar
reminder
system
operates
irrespective of
whether Money is
currently running.**

The reminder icon has two incarnations in the Task Bar, and
one in the Payment Reminder dialog (see the figure below):

Reminders are due

You have inspected the reminders (i.e. you have
carried out step 1 or 2 below)

Reminders are overdue (see the Remember tip)

Double-click the first icon to view the reminders. After
you've inspected them, do one of the following:

2 Click here to close the dialog

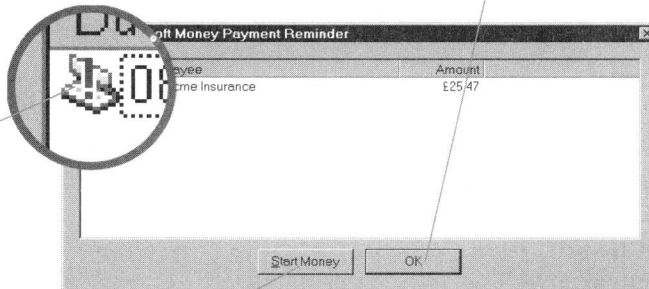

REMEMBER

**The icon
here:
indicates
that the
reminder is overdue.**

Click here to launch Money (with the
Payment Calendar displayed) and enter
the transactions immediately

For what to do after step 1, see pages 83-84.

Customising reminders

You can customise the following reminder aspects:

- the amount of notice in the Payment Calendar reminder system

- whether or not the Task Bar reminder system is operational

Setting the Payment Calendar notice period

By default, the Payment Calendar reminds you about pending transactions up to 10 days before they're due. If you want to change this, pull down the Tools menu and click Options. Carry out the following steps:

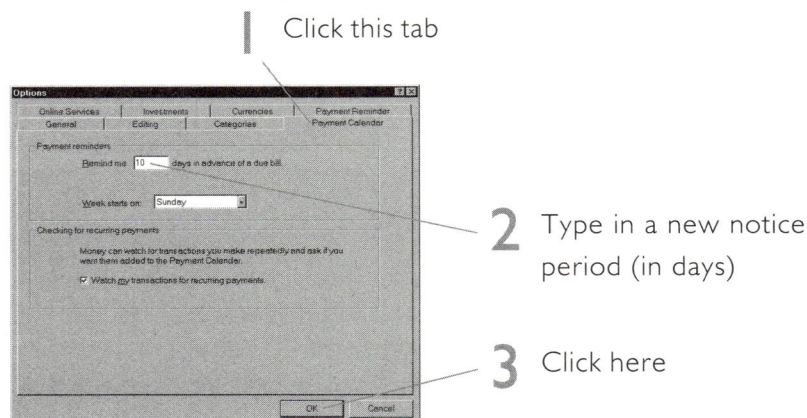

Click this tab

2 Type in a new notice period (in days)

3 Click here

Deactivating the Task Bar reminder

Right-click the Reminder icon (whatever its incarnation) in the Windows Task Bar. Then do the following:

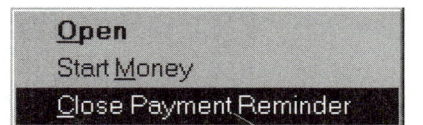

Click here

HANDY TIP

If you want to reactivate the Task Bar reminder system, pull down the Tools menu and click Options. Click the Payment Reminder tab. Select Use the Payment Reminder. Click OK.

Entering scheduled transactions (1)

When you've received a reminder, and responded to it either by:

- carrying out step 1 on page 80; or

- carrying out step 1 on page 81

you can use the Payment Calendar to enter one or more of the outstanding transactions into the Account Register. To help you do this, the Payment Calendar has a very useful in-built calendar.

Using the Payment Calendar's in-built calendar

You can use the in-built calendar to determine which dates have pending transactions (🖅 displays against them). You can also do any of the following:

HANDY TIP **You can use the procedures discussed here and on page 84 to enter standing order or direct debit transactions.**

HANDY TIP **Follow step 4 for a helpful overview of the current year, and 5 to narrow down the focus to a specific month (after this, the calendar reverts to the original view format).**

REMEMBER **If you carry out step 4, steps 1 and 2 have the effect of advancing the calendar in annual – as opposed to monthly – jumps.**

1 Click here to view the previous month

2 Click here to view the next month

3 Click a date to select associated transactions in the Payment Calendar

4 Click here

5 Click a box to view the relevant month

Entering scheduled transactions (2)

Now carry out the following steps:

REMEMBER

Re step 1 – to select a transaction for inclusion into the Register, click: ☐
The result is: ☑

Select the transaction(s) you want to insert into the Register

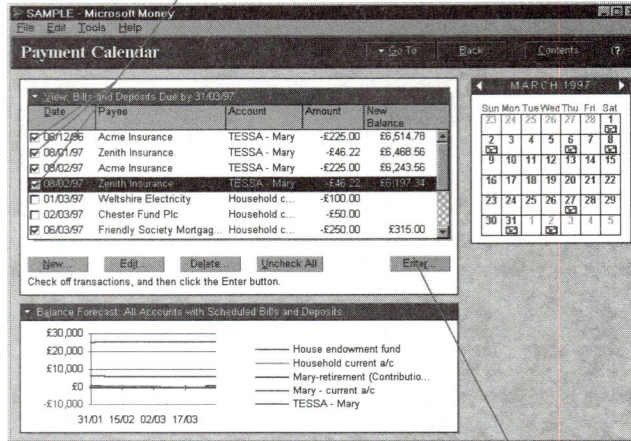

REMEMBER

Ensure the New Balance field shows a large enough balance to meet the transaction. If it doesn't, alter the transaction amount in the form before you carry out step 3.

2 Click here

3 Click here

HANDY TIP

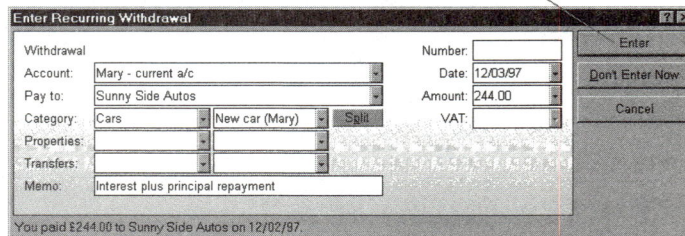

If you want to revise the schedule details for just this instalment of the transaction (see page 78), amend any of the fields in the form *before* you carry out step 3.

Multiple selections

If you select more than one transaction in step 1, Money launches successive versions of this form. Follow step 3 for each.

Reconciliation

Use this chapter to learn how to 'reconcile' (harmonise) your accounts with your bank statements. You'll use various techniques to compare deposits and withdrawals against statement entries, and isolate any discrepancies. Once located, inconsistencies can be adjusted easily and conveniently, or – if small – written off. Finally, you'll confirm that reconciliation is complete.

Covers

Reconciliation – an overview 86

Reconciliation – stage one 88

Reconciliation – stage two 91

Reconciliation – stage three 95

Reconciliation – stage four 97

Reconciliation – an overview (1)

Money accounts have to be 'reconciled' against records kept by your bank or building society, in order to ensure that no inaccuracies creep in. You should do this every time you receive a bank statement. (If, for any reason, you omit to do this for one or more statements, you must rectify this *before* attempting to reconcile a later statement.)

REMEMBER

Because bank accounts have more variables than building society accounts (e.g. there are bank charges to be taken into account), we'll concentrate on them in this section.

In essence, reconciliation simply involves verifying that transactions in your account match those in your bank statement (or passbook). This is usually a simple and straightforward procedure, though, because Money guides you through every stage, ensuring that no mathematical errors infiltrate the process.

In rather more detail, however, reconciliation is the process of:

1.   transferring bank statement information (for example, bank charges and interest payments) into the corresponding Money account

2.   comparing the bank statement with the account and marking as 'reconciled' those transactions which are identical in both

3.   totalling the number of cleared items in both the statement and account, and making sure the two totals tally

4.   resolving any instances where the statement and account *don't* tally

It is, however, important to bear in mind that you won't necessarily perform all 4 steps. For example, in many cases steps 3 and 4 will be unnecessary because the process of comparing your account and bank statement (steps 1 and 2 above) discloses no discrepancies.

This is the ideal.

Reconciliation – an overview (2)

Additionally, the order in which you carry out steps 1-4 on page 86 may vary. As an example of this, Money lets you manually correct any discrepancies you find:

- in the early stages of reconciliation

OR

- in the final stage

You can choose whichever approach is the most convenient and useful.

Initial reconciliation

Normally, reconciliation is straightforward enough. However, when you reconcile an account for the first time, the situation can become slightly more complex. This is because the initial setting up of an account involves inserting, as the opening balance, the balance on your latest statement.

This is all well and good provided that the figure you inserted was correct i.e. there were no outstanding transactions (withdrawals or deposits which hadn't yet appeared on the statement) at the time. If, however, the process of reconciling the account demonstrates that there were, you have the following options:

- adjusting the opening balance (through inserting into your account any transactions which were omitted originally)

- allowing Money to make its own adjustment at the end of reconciliation (see page 102)

The first method is most often required.

Reconciliation – stage one (1)

In the Contents area, carry out the following steps:

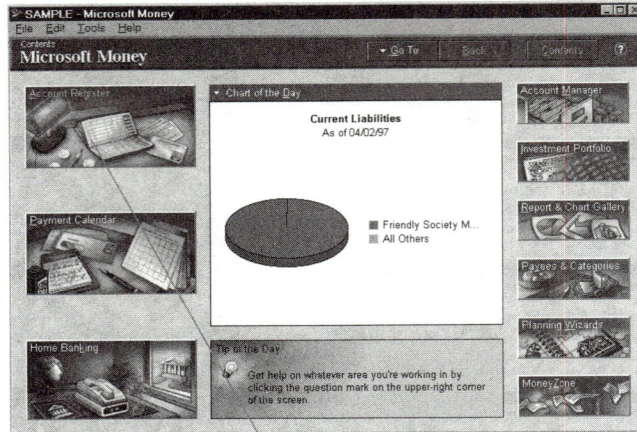

Click here

Now do the following:

2 Click here

		C	Payment	Deposit	Balance
Friendly Society Mortg Liability					
House endowment fund					
House Value (estimate)			15.00		669.00
Household current a/c			244.00		425.00
Household savings a/c			21.00		404.00
John's Portfolio			10.00		394.00
John - Credit Card				1,172.00	1,566.00
John - current a/c			461.00		1,105.00
John - private pensions			500.00		605.00
John - pension (Contributions)			10.00		595.00
John - tax set aside			244.00		351.00
Mary's Portfolio				1,172.00	1,523.00
Mary - Credit Card			119.00		1,404.00
• Mary - current a/c			20.00		1,384.00
Mary - retirement			244.00		1,140.00
Mary-retirement (Contributions)				1,172.00	2,312.00
PEP account			20.00		2,292.00
Sarah's current account			1,000.00		1,292.00
Sarah's Eco Fund			257.00		1,035.00
TESSA - Mary					
EEpay 06/02/97			450.00		585.00
dd 12/02/97	Sunny Side Autos		244.00		341.00
27/02/97	Baldens PR Ltd			1,172.00	1,513.00
XXfer 27/02/97			1,000.00		513.00
EEpay 28/02/97	Credit Ltd		307.00		206.00
				Ending Balance:	£206.00

3 Click the account you
want to reconcile

Reconciliation – stage one (2)

Now carry out the following steps:

Click here

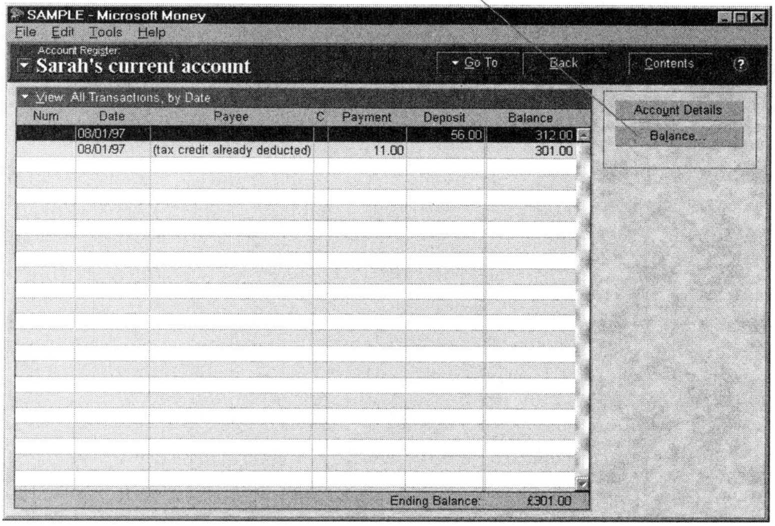

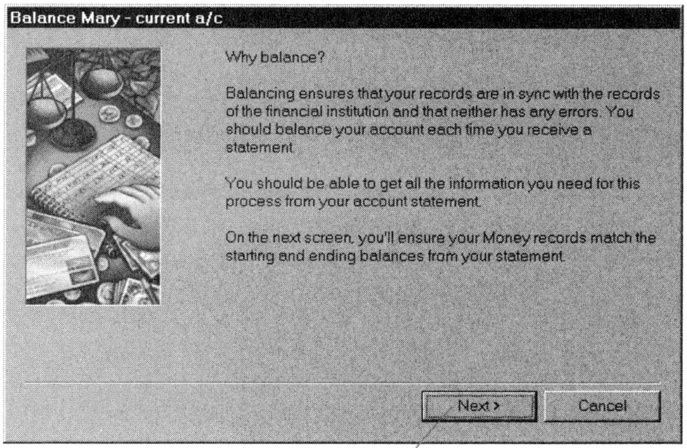

2 Click here

Reconciliation – stage one (3)

Now carry out steps 1-3 and 5 below. Additionally, you should follow steps 4 and 6 if you want to allocate a category/sub-category combination to the interest and/or bank charge entries.

Finally, perform step 7 to initiate the reconciliation process:

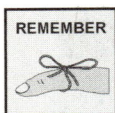

REMEMBER

Step 1 should only apply to accounts which are being reconciled for the first time.

1 If this figure *isn't* your statement's opening balance, type it in

2 Insert the statement's final balance

3 Insert any service charges

Balance Sarah's current account

Enter the following information from your statement:

Statement date: 28/02/97
Starting balance: 256.00
Ending balance: 301.00

If applicable, also enter the following:

Service charge:
Category:
Interest earned:
Category:

Next >   Cancel

4 Apply a category/ sub- category

REMEMBER

Before you carry out step 7, type in the final date covered by the statement in the Statement date field:

Statement date: 28/02/97

5 Insert any interest payments

7 Click here

6 Apply a category/ sub-category

In the next stage of the reconciliation process, you inspect all relevant deposits and withdrawals in your account and compare them with the equivalent transaction entries on your statement.

See page 91.

Reconciliation – stage two (1)

After step 7 on page 90, Money re-launches the Account Manager, but with an additional component: the Balance Account side-bar. You use this to compare entries on your statement with those in the account. This is a crucial component of the reconciliation process. Fortunately, Money makes it easy and convenient.

Even more helpfully, in the normal course of events the entries will correspond exactly – the ideal situation. When this is the case, you tell Money as much and each ratified transaction is marked with:

C

in the C ('Cleared') field. Each time you ratify a transaction, Money adjusts the running totals near the base of the side-bar.

The illustration below provides definitions of the three totals:

See page 95 for how to use this.

HANDY TIP

Money also adjusts further totals in the Balance Account side-bar:

Cleared so far:	
0 Deposits	0.00
1 Payments	-20.00

The opening account balance – as you ratify entries, Money adjusts this figure

Cleared:	630.00
Statement:	842.99
Difference:	-212.99

This field is updated as reconciliation proceeds. Reconciliation is complete when it shows: 0.00

The final statement balance

For what to do if the Difference field *doesn't* register 0.00 after reconciliation, see page 97.

Reconciling – stage two (2)

Now carry out step 1 below. Repeat for all relevant transactions within the account. Follow step 2 if, at the end of this stage, the Difference field (near the base of the side-bar) shows:

0.00

Balance Account
side-bar

HANDY TIP **You may well not be able to clear *all* transactions at this stage. If you encounter a transaction which was entered incorrectly and needs amending, or if you need to add a new one, you can do so now (before you carry out step 2), if you want. See pages 93-94.**

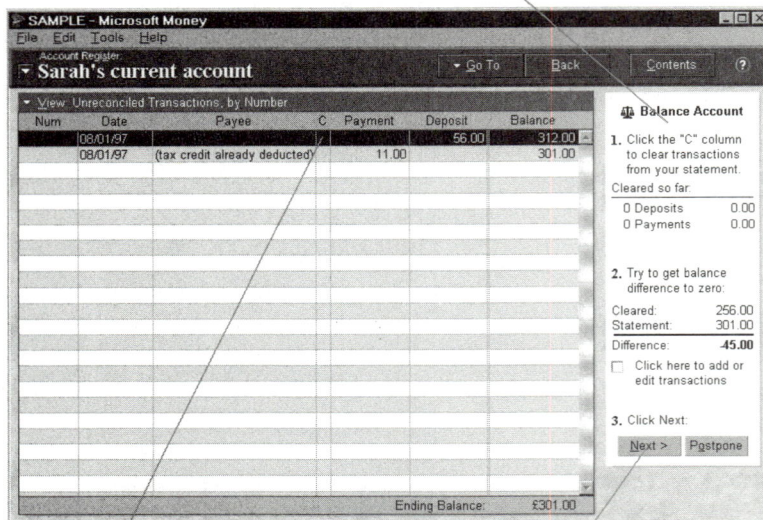

1 Click here in entries which have an exact equivalent in your statement

2 Click here

If, when all transactions have been ratified, the Difference field doesn't show 0.00, *don't* (at this stage) carry out step 2.

Instead, refer to page 97.

Reconciliation – stage two (3)

If you find transactions which don't match entries in your statement, there are two possible explanations:

A. The fault lies with your bank, in that it has entered one or more transactions wrongly. All you can do in this situation is contact the bank and get it to correct the error. In the interim, don't mark the relevant transaction as cleared.

B. *You* have entered one or more transactions wrongly. Or you haven't entered one or more transactions which appear on the statement and which are correct (for example, a salary deposit). In either case, you can easily rectify the problem yourself.

Resolving situation ß

Follow steps 1 and 2 to amend an existing transaction, or just 2 to enter a new one.

HANDY TIP **If you want, you can defer carrying out the procedures described here and on pages 94 & 95 until later. Simply carry out step 2 on page 92 and jump to page 97.**

REMEMBER **If you do carry out the procedures described here and on pages 94 & 95, they should be implemented *before* you carry out step 2 on page 92.**

Click a transaction which needs to be revised

2 Click here

Reconciliation – stage two (4)

Now carry out either of the following steps:

1 Click here to add a
new transaction

If you want, you can defer carrying out the procedures described here and on pages 93 & 95 until later. Simply carry out step 2 on page 92 and jump to page 97.

2 Click here to edit the transaction
selected in step 1 on page 93

If you do carry out the procedures described here and on pages 93 & 95, they should be implemented *before* you carry out step 2 on page 92.

Perform the following steps:

4 Click here

3 Complete or amend
the appropriate fields

Reconciliation – stage three (1)

You can use two further aids at this stage of the reconciliation process. The first is the simplest, and often the most effective. Count the number of deposits in your statement, then compare this with the following field in the Balance Account side-bar:

```
Cleared so far:
  0 Deposits          0.00
  1 Payments        -20.00
```

Compare this number with the total number of deposits in your account

REMEMBER

Ideally, carry out these suggestions *before* you follow the procedures on pages 93-94.

Or leave them till later and jump to page 97.

Now compare the total number of withdrawals with the following:

```
Cleared so far:
  0 Deposits          0.00
  1 Payments        -20.00
```

Compare this number with the total number of withdrawals in your account

You should also total deposit and withdrawal amounts on your statement. Compare these with the totals shown to the right of the fields mentioned above.

Finally, carry out step 2 on page 92.

Reconciliation – stage three (2)

You've just carried out step 2 on page 92. If you did so when the Difference field in the Balance Account side-bar showed 0.00:

HANDY TIP

If you've followed the procedures so far (including step 2 on page 92) *without the Difference field showing 0.00,* **reconciliation isn't yet complete.**

Go to page 97 and proceed from there.

Cleared:	301.00
Statement:	301.00
Difference:	**0.00**

There are no 'rogue' transactions

this signifies that – in respect of the selected account – the reconciliation process is almost complete.

To complete it, do the following:

Balance Account

Congratulations!

You have balanced your 'Sarah's current account' account through 28/02/97.

Finish   Cancel

Click here

HANDY TIP

Another result of a successful account reconciliation is that reconciled transactions now show:

R

in the C (Cleared) field in the Account Register, instead of:

C

To show that reconciliation is complete, Money displays a message in the side-bar:

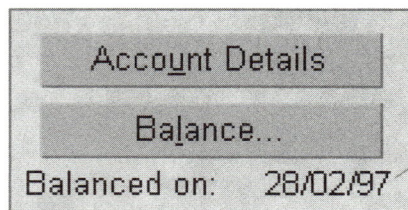

Account Details

Balance...

Balanced on: 28/02/97

The account has been reconciled

Reconciliation – stage four (1)

You've just carried out step 2 on page 92. If you did so without achieving the situation where the Difference field in the Balance Account side-bar shows 0.00, reconciliation is incomplete. You need to take further action.

Money offers you three further alternatives which you can use to resolve the situation:

Editing – you can return to the account (complete with the Balance Account side-bar) and make another attempt to find and correct the discrepancy. This is also useful in two additional situations:

A. if – at an earlier stage in the reconciliation process – you deferred adjusting incorrect transactions, or adding new transactions which were present on your statement but had been missed off your account (see the Handy Tip on page 93)

B. if this is the first time you've reconciled your account and if, when you set it up, there were outstanding transactions which hadn't yet been cleared

AutoReconcile – this is a special feature which you can run to have Money attempt to find the transaction(s) causing the problem. (If this doesn't work, you can always return to either or both of the other techniques.)

Automatic balancing – use this as a last resort. If neither you nor Money's AutoReconcile feature can locate the discrepancy, you can have Money amend the overall account balance for you by inserting an internal adjustment.

These alternatives are covered in detail on the following pages.

Reconciliation – stage four (2)

Editing

After following step 2 on page 92 (without the Difference field in the Balance Account side-bar showing 0.00), carry out the following steps:

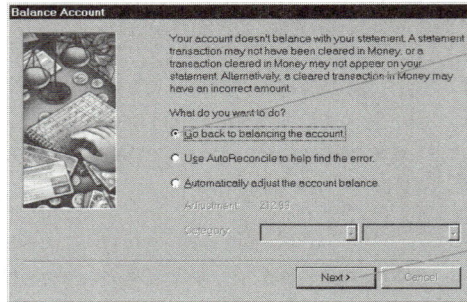

| Click here

2 Click here

Money returns you to your account. Do the following:

3 Click a transaction which needs to be revised

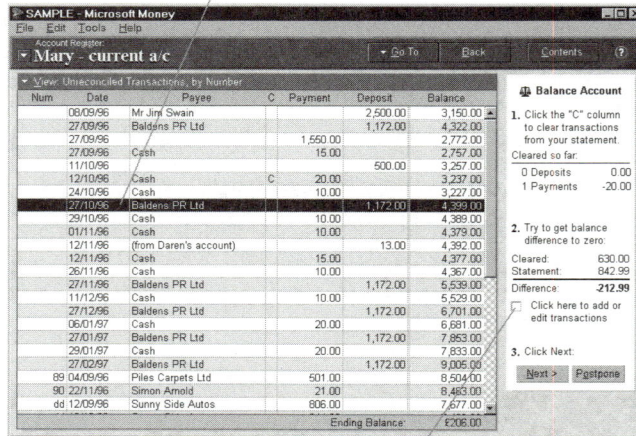

4 Click here

Reconciliation – stage four (3)

Now carry out ONE of the following steps:

1 | Click here to add a new transaction

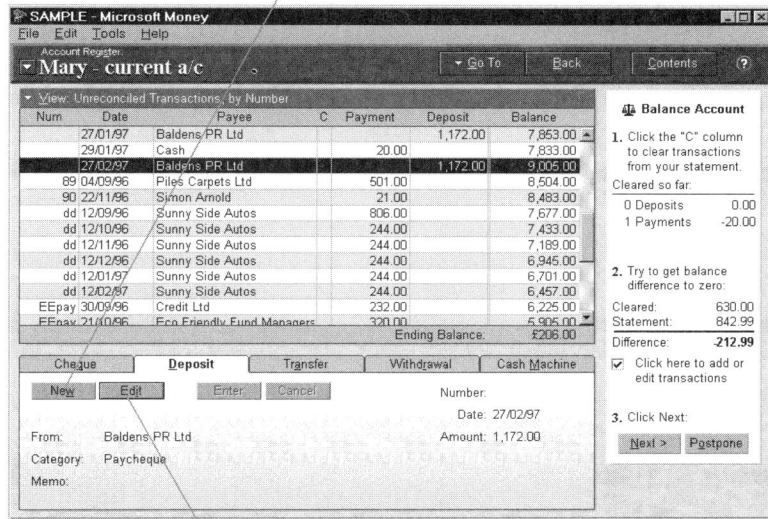

2 Click here to edit the transaction
selected in step 3 on page 98

Perform the following steps:

4 Click here

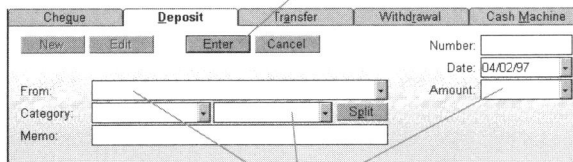

3 Complete the appropriate fields

Reconciliation – stage four (4)

Using AutoReconcile

After following step 2 on page 92 (without the Difference field in the Balance Account side-bar showing 0.00), carry out the following steps:

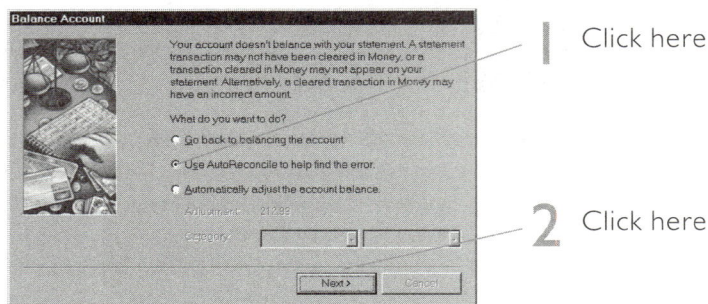

1 Click here

2 Click here

After this, one of two things can happen.

A. If AutoReconcile is successful

If AutoReconcile believes it has located the discrepancy, a message similar to this launches:

3 Click here

HANDY TIP

In this instance, Money is suggesting that a transaction has been incorrectly entered as a withdrawal rather than a deposit.

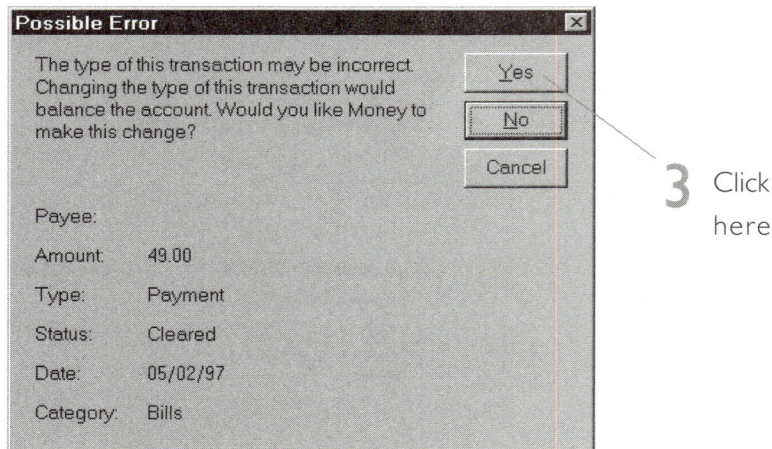

If AutoReconcile's suggestion is correct, follow step 3 above to have Money make the necessary correction.

Reconciliation – stage four (5)

If the suggested course of action *isn't* right, don't follow step 3 on page 100. Instead, click the No button in the Possible Error dialog:

After this, Money may produce another suggestion. If this is right, follow step 3 on page 100. If not, click the No button.

If no suggestion is correct, see 'B. If AutoReconcile isn't successful' below.

B. If AutoReconcile isn't successful

If AutoReconcile is unable to come up with any suggestions as to the discrepancy between your account and statement, or when it runs out of suggestions, another message appears.

Carry out the following:

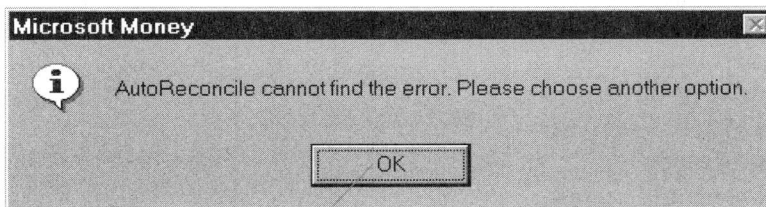

Click here

Money now returns you to the Balance Account dialog shown on page 100.

Follow either of the other two alternative methods to complete reconciliation.

Reconciliation – stage four (6)

Automatic balancing

If all other attempts to locate the discrepancy between your statement and account have failed, carry out the following steps after following step 2 on page 92:

BEWARE

Having Money adjust the final balance by the amount of the discrepancy is a technique you may well want to limit to instances where the shortfall is only slight, and can therefore be written off with impunity.

For cases where the discrepancy is large and relates to one or more transactions, it's advisable to rely on the methods discussed on pages 98-101.

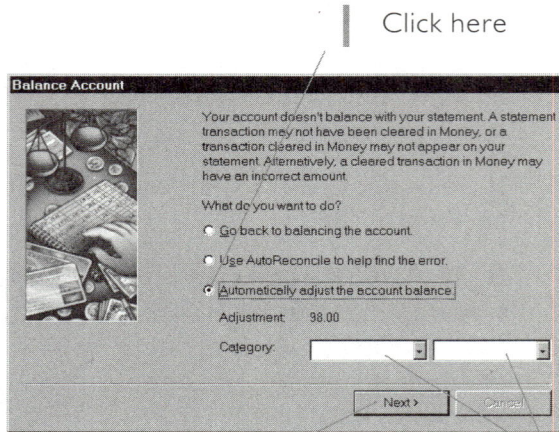

Click here

3 Click here

2 Optional – apply a category/sub-category combination

The final result

Whichever of the methods discussed on pages 98-102 you used to complete reconciliation, the following dialog launches. Do the following:

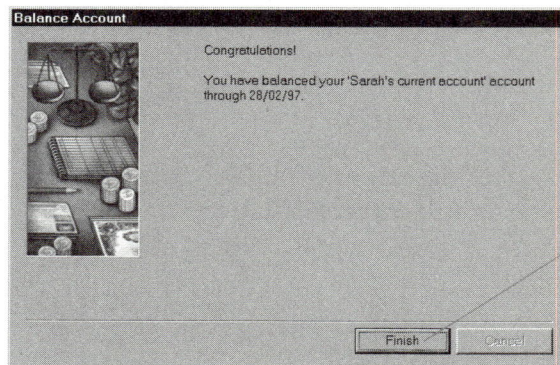

Click here

Reports and Charts

Use this chapter to view your financial data as reports and charts. You'll create standardised reports and charts, and then learn how to customise them very specifically by stipulating which transactions display. You'll save customised reports and charts as Favourites, for easy retrieval later. Finally, you'll print your report/chart.

Covers

Reports and charts – an overview 104

Report/chart types 106

Creating a standard report 108

Customising reports 110

Getting ready to print reports 115

Report printing 116

Creating a standard chart 117

Customising charts 119

Working with charts 125

Chart printing 126

Reports and charts – an overview (1)

Money makes managing your day-to-day finances easy. However, it's also vital to be able to take an overview of them. You can do this in two ways:

- textually, by generating reports

- visually, by generating charts

Use Money's report formats to achieve a detailed written evaluation of your finances, based on the heading you select. Utilise its charting capability to make a similar kind of evaluation *instantly*. Better still, use both reports and charts for a comprehensive picture of how your finances are progressing.

A sample report

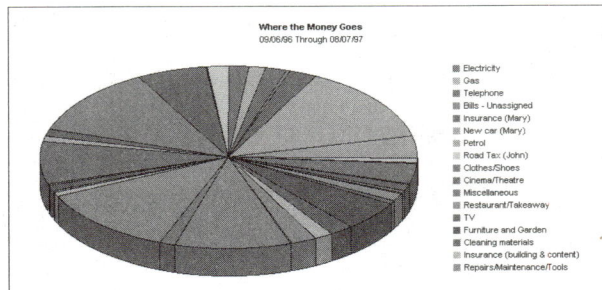

A sample chart

Reports and charts – an overview (2)

You generate reports and charts from within a special area known as the Report & Chart Gallery.

Money makes the entire process very easy and straightforward by regarding reports and charts as different ways of looking at the same data (which they undoubtedly are). Once you've created a report or chart, you can do either or both of the following:

- customise it very specifically, to take account of your precise requirements

- save frequently-used reports and charts as 'Favourites' in a common location, so that you can refer to them very rapidly and conveniently

Using a combination of the above results in a very powerful technique for data inspection, and one which can save a considerable amount of time and effort.

For example, you could customise a chart by stipulating:

-   which account(s) are included

-   which categories/sub-categories are included

-   the chart type

-   whether it displays in 3D

-   the font used

-   the date range within which transactions are included

and then save it as a Favourite. Rather than recreate this chart again (a relatively long-winded task), you can simply recall it with a few mouse clicks...

Report/chart types (1)

Money provides a large number of report/chart types. (In their uncustomised forms, they're particularly easy to apply).

In Money, reports and charts fall under the following headings:

Not all reports have a chart equivalent.

- Spending Habits

- What I Have

- What I Owe

- Investments

- Taxes

- Favourites

A special chart – the Balance Forecaster Graph – displays in the Payment Calendar:

These are further subdivided as follows:

This chart displays your projected balance over the coming months. To extend or restrict the balance period, use the inbuilt calendar. (See steps 1 and 2 on page 83 for how to do this.)

Spending Habits	Where the Money Goes
	Who is Getting My Money
	Monthly Cash Flow
	Account Transactions
	Income Vs. Spending
	My Budget
	How I'm Doing on My Budget
What I Have	Net Worth
	Account Balances
	Account Balance History
	Account Details

Report/chart types (2)

Not all reports have a chart equivalent.

Money displays a special Chart of the Day in the Contents area:

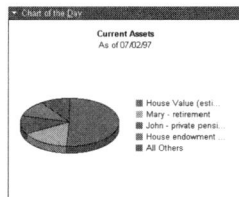

Out of 5 common chart types, Money displays 1 at random each day.

What I Owe	Upcoming Bills
	Upcoming Bills and Deposits This Month
	Credit Card Debt
	Loan Terms
	Loan Amortisation
Investments	Portfolio Value by Investment Account
	Portfolio Value by Investment Type
	Performance by Investment Account
	Performance by Investment Type
	Price History
	Investment Transaction
Taxes	Tax-related Transactions
	Capital Gains
	Loan Interest
	Tax Software Report
	Value Added Tax – VAT Rate
	Value Added Tax – Category
Favourites	Reports and charts you store for future use are located under this heading

Creating a standard report (1)

To have Money compile a report for you, do the following in the Contents area:

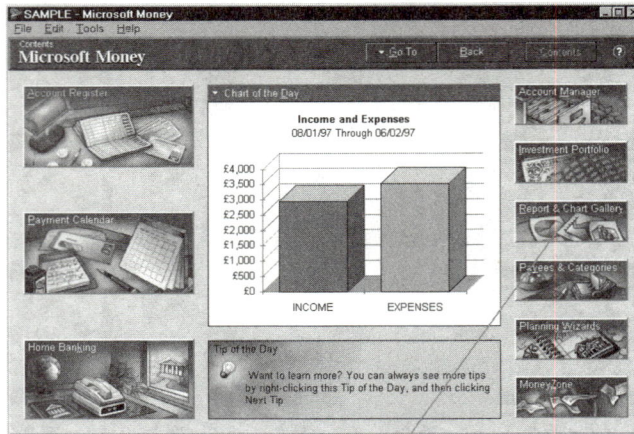

| Click here

Now do the following:

HANDY TIP

Money provides a brief description of the type/sub-type here:

2 Click an overall report type

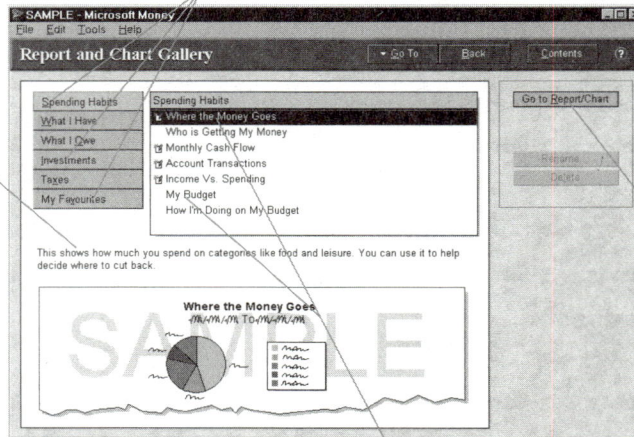

HANDY TIP

Re step 3 – report sub-types which have ☑ **against them can also be viewed as charts. See pages 117-118.**

4 Click here

3 Click a report sub-type

Creating a standard report (2)

Now do the following:

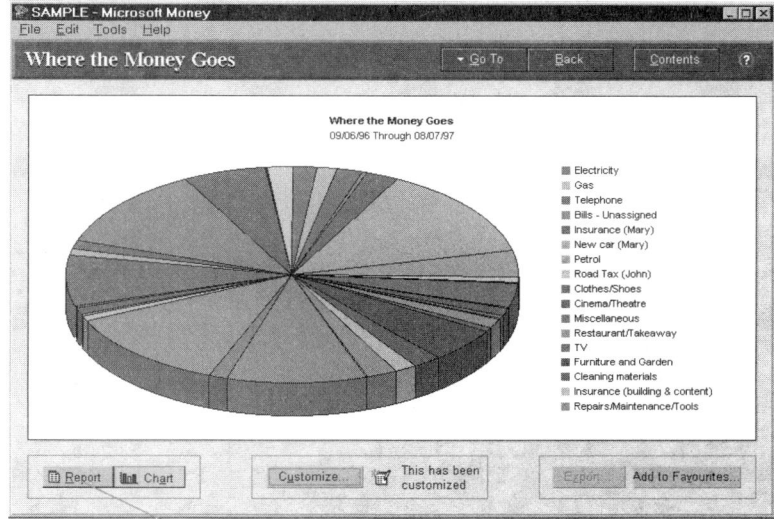

If Money is currently displaying
a chart, click here

The
equivalent
report

Customising reports (1)

The procedures on pages 108 and 109 produce standardised reports. These are adequate for most purposes. However, when you become more experienced with Money you may well want to exercise more control.

You can:

HANDY TIP **To save a report you've fine-tuned as a Favourite, click the Add to Favourites button in the Report window. Do the following:**

2 Click here

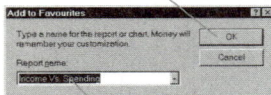

Name the report

- specify the report title

- specify the column headings

- specify the basis Money uses for displaying rows

- specify preset column widths

- specify which typeface/type size a report displays and prints in

- have transactions under a specifiable value (expressed as a percentage of the total value) combined into one (for cleaner looking reports)

- have rows sorted in descending order according to amount, rather then alphabetically (the default)

HANDY TIP **To return to a 'Favourite' report, click the My Favourites button in the Report & Chart Gallery. Select the report in the list of report sub-types. Click the Go to Report/Chart button.**

- specify dates or date ranges as requirements for the inclusion of transactions

- include/exclude specific accounts

- specify which transactions are included, according to:

  – what text is in the fields

  – the transaction type

  – the payee (if any) to which transactions relate

  – which category or categories are associated with transactions

Customising reports (2)

Carry out the following after creating a standard report:

Click
here

HANDY TIP

**Re step 7 –
if you want
to limit the
report to
more than one
account, click
Multiple Accounts
in the list which
appears. Now do
the following:**

Now perform steps 2-7 below, as appropriate (5 and 6 are alternatives). Finally, carry out step 8:

2 Click the relevant
accounts

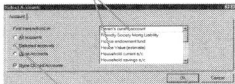

1 Click
here

3 Click
here

**Finally, carry out
step 8.**

2 Name the
report

3 Click here; choose
a row basis

8 Click
here

4 Click
here;
click a
column
heading

6 Type in start
and end dates

5 Click here; click
a date range

7 Click here; select
an account

Customising reports (3)

HANDY TIP

To have rows sorted by amount (rather than alphabetically), click here:

Applying a new typeface/type size

Generate a standard report (see pages 108-109), then follow step 1 on page 111. Now carry out steps 1-4 below, as appropriate. Finally, perform step 5 to view the report:

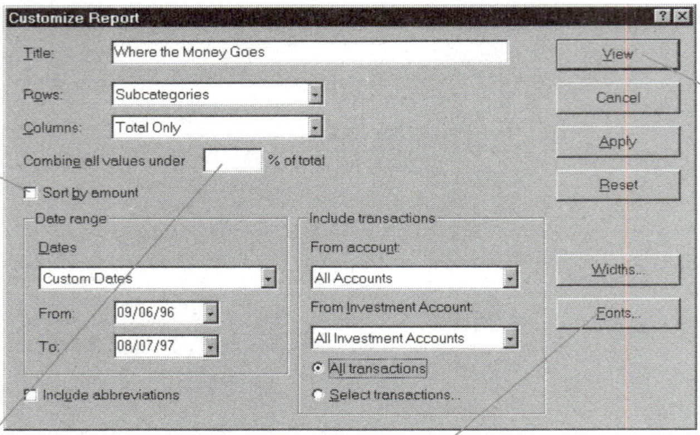

HANDY TIP

To have low-value entries combined into one, enter a percentage of the total value here: (e.g. to lump together entries below £250 in an account whose maximum amount is £5000, enter 5%).

Customize Report

Title: Where the Money Goes

Rows: Subcategories

Columns: Total Only

Combing all values under [ ] % of total

☐ Sort by amount

Date range

Dates: Custom Dates

From: 09/06/96

To: 08/07/97

☐ Include abbreviations

Include transactions

From account: All Accounts

From Investment Account: All Investment Accounts

◉ All transactions

○ Select transactions...

View | Cancel | Apply | Reset | Widths... | Fonts...

5 Click here

| Click here

2 Click a font

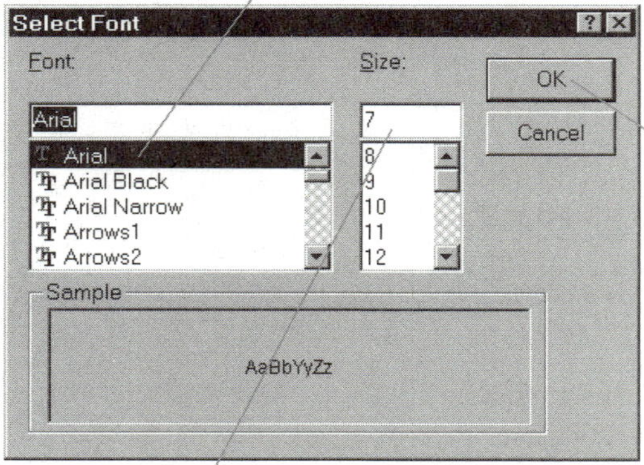

Select Font

Font: Arial

- Arial
- Arial Black
- Arial Narrow
- Arrows1
- Arrows2

Size: 7

- 8
- 9
- 10
- 11
- 12

OK | Cancel

4 Click here

Sample

AaBbYyZz

3 Enter a type size

Customising reports (4)

Specifying a preset column width

Generate a standard report (see pages 108-109), then follow step 1 on page 111. Now carry out steps 1-3 below, as appropriate. Finally, perform step 4 to view the report:

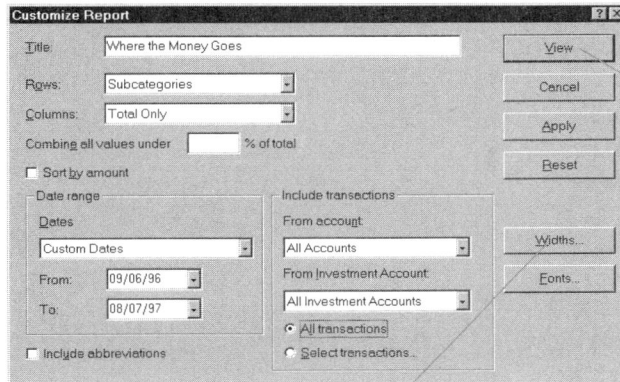

4 Click here

Click here

2 Click a width setting

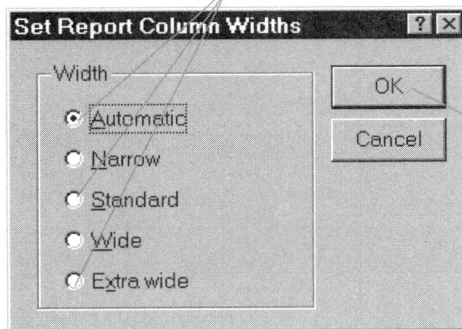

3 Click here

Customising reports (5)

Specifying which transactions are included

Generate a standard report (see pages 108-109), then follow step 1 on page 111. Now carry out steps 1-3 below, as appropriate. Finally, perform step 4 to view the report:

(see pages 108-109)

HANDY TIP

Re step 2 – to limit the report to specific transaction types, click the Details tab. Click the Transaction type arrow; in the list, click a type. Now follow steps 3 & 4.

HANDY TIP

Re step 2 – to limit the report to specific payees, click the Payee tab. Click the Selected payees field; in the list, click 1 or more payees. Now follow steps 3 & 4.

HANDY TIP

Re step 2 – to limit the report to specific categories, click the Categories tab. Click Selected categories; in the list, click 1 or more categories. Now follow steps 3 & 4.

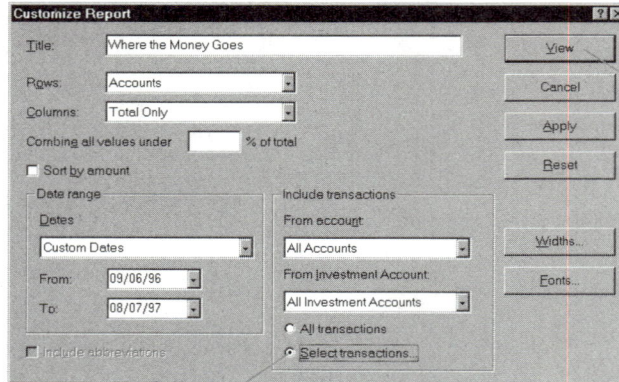

Customize Report
Title: Where the Money Goes
Rows: Accounts
Columns: Total Only
Combine all values under ____ % of total
☐ Sort by amount
Date range — Dates: Custom Dates — From: 09/06/96 — To: 08/07/97 — ☐ Include abbreviations
Include transactions — From account: All Accounts — From Investment Account: All Investment Accounts — ○ All transactions — ◉ Select transactions...
View · Cancel · Apply · Reset · Widths... · Fonts...

4 Click here

Click here

2 Type in text to have the report limited to fields which contain it

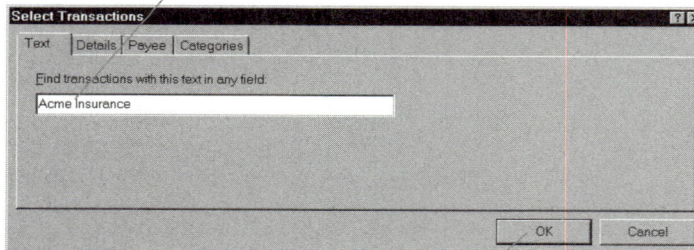

Select Transactions
Text │ Details │ Payee │ Categories
Find transactions with this text in any field.
Acme Insurance
OK · Cancel

3 Click here

Getting ready to print reports

It's often helpful to print out reports. However, before you can do this you need to:

- make sure the correct printer is selected

- specify a page size

- specify a page orientation (see below for a definition):

Portrait    Landscape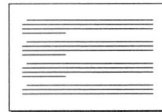

- make sure your printer's internal settings are adjusted correctly

Report setup

Pull down the File menu and click Print Setup. Now carry out steps 1-3, as appropriate. Finally, perform step 4.

Click here; select a printer from the list

 **Click the Properties button to adjust your printer's internal settings (for how to do this, see your printer's manual). Finally, follow step 4.**

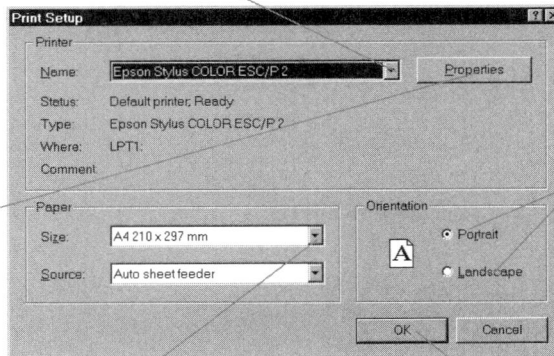

3 Choose an orientation

2 Click here; choose a page size in the list

4 Click here

Report printing

Once you've generated and/or customised a report, you can print it out.

Printing a report

Pull down the File menu and do the following:

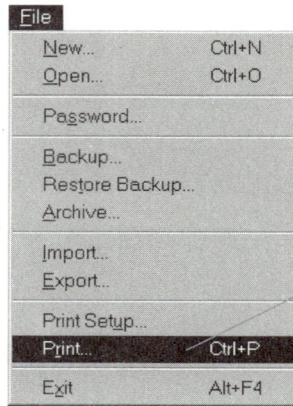

File	
New...	Ctrl+N
Open...	Ctrl+O
Password...	
Backup...	
Restore Backup...	
Archive...	
Import...	
Export...	
Print Setup...	
Print...	Ctrl+P
Exit	Alt+F4

Click here

HANDY TIP

If you need to adjust your printer's internal settings, click the Setup button:

Setup...

Then follow steps 1-4 (as appropriate) on page 115.

REMEMBER

Re step 3 – the available quality options depend on the selected printer.

2 Optional – enter start and end page numbers

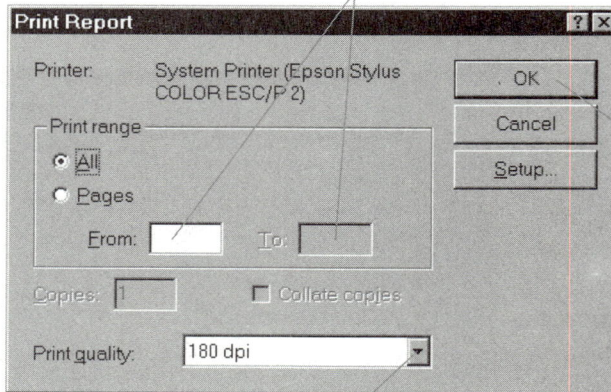

Print Report

Printer:	System Printer (Epson Stylus COLOR ESC/P 2)

Print range
- (•) All
- ( ) Pages

From: [ ]   To: [ ]

Copies: [1]   ☐ Collate copies

Print quality: [180 dpi ▼]

OK

Cancel

Setup...

4 Click here

3 Click here; select a print quality in the list

Creating a standard chart (1)

Use charts to achieve a very useful visual overview of your finances.

Viewing a chart

In the Contents area, do the following:

REMEMBER **Many of Money's report types (see pages 106-107) have a chart associated with them.**

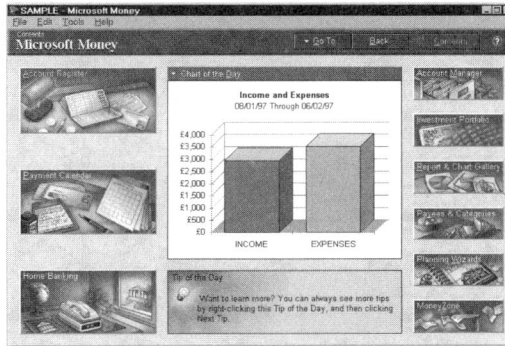

Click here

Now perform the following steps:

HANDY TIP **Money provides a brief description of the type/sub-type here:**

2 Click an overall chart type

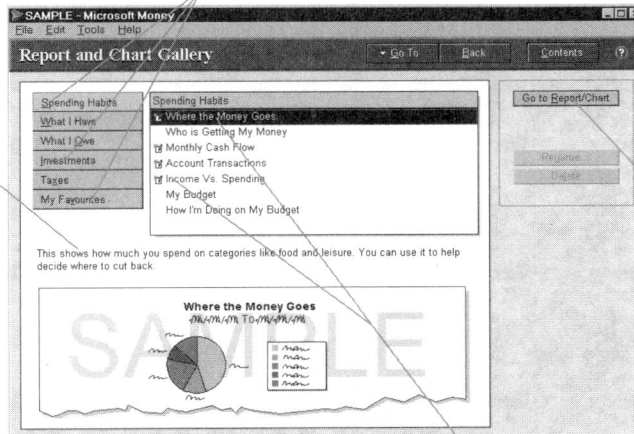

HANDY TIP **Re step 3 – not all reports have charts associated with them.**

4 Click here

3 Click a chart sub-type

Creating a standard chart (2)

Now do the following (if appropriate):

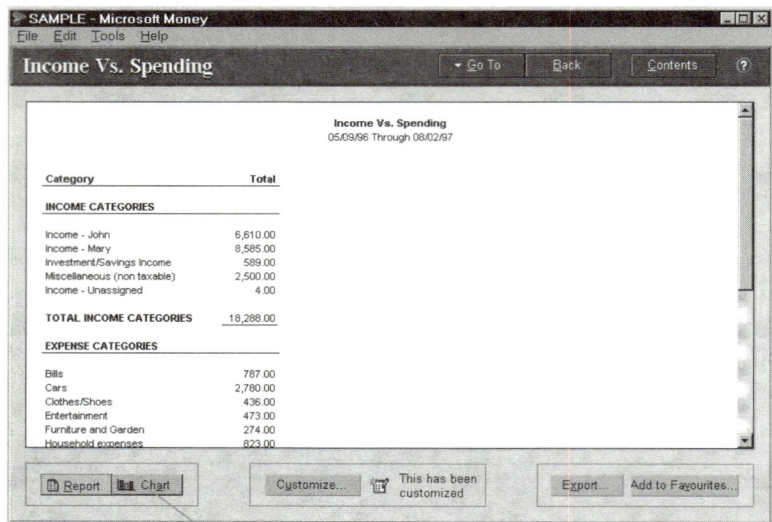

If Money is currently displaying
a report, click here

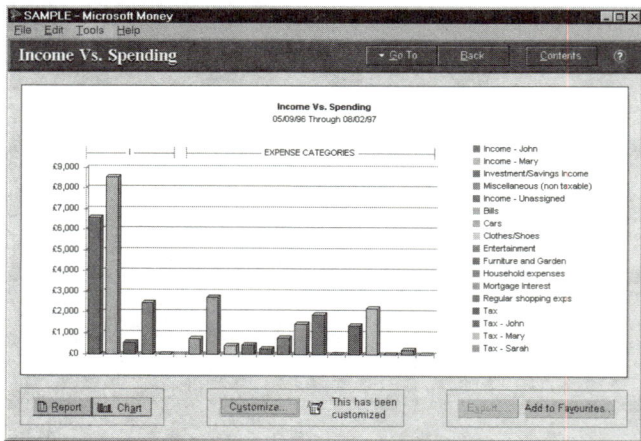

The
equivalent
chart

Customising charts (1)

The procedures on pages 117-118 produce standardised charts. These are adequate for most purposes. However, when you become more experienced with Money you may well want to exercise more control.

You can:

HANDY TIP

To save a chart you've fine-tuned as a Favourite, click the Add to Favourites button in the Chart window. Do the following:

2 Click here

Add to Favourites

Type a name for the report or chart. Money will remember your customization.

OK

Cancel

Report name:

Income Vs. Spending

1 Name the chart

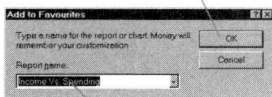

- specify the chart type. Available options are:
  - Bar
  - Line
  - Pie

- specify the chart title and column headings

- specify the basis Money uses for displaying rows

- specify which typeface/type size text within a chart displays and prints in

- have transactions under a specifiable value (expressed as a percentage of the total value) combined into one (for cleaner looking charts)

- have rows sorted in descending order according to amount, rather then alphabetically (the default)

HANDY TIP

To return to a 'Favourite' chart, click the My Favourites button in the Report & Chart Gallery. Select the chart in the list of chart sub-types. Click the Go to Report/Chart button.

- specify dates or date ranges as requirements for the inclusion of transactions

- include/exclude specific accounts

- specify which transactions are included, according to:
  - what text is in the fields
  - the transaction type
  - the payee (if any) to which transactions relate
  - which category or categories are associated with transactions

Customising charts (2)

Applying a chart type

Carry out the following steps after creating a standard chart:

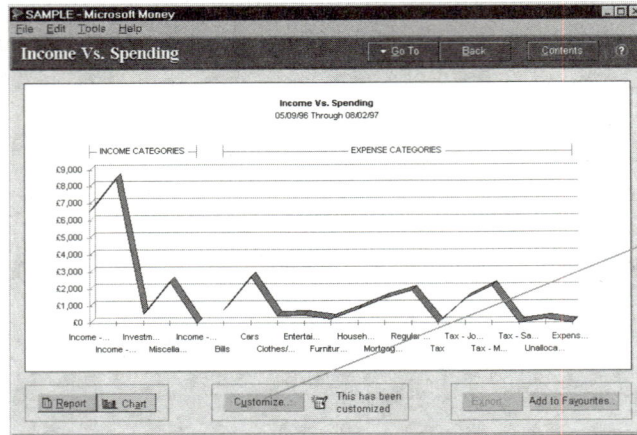

| Click
here

Now perform steps 2-3 below:

2 Click a chart type

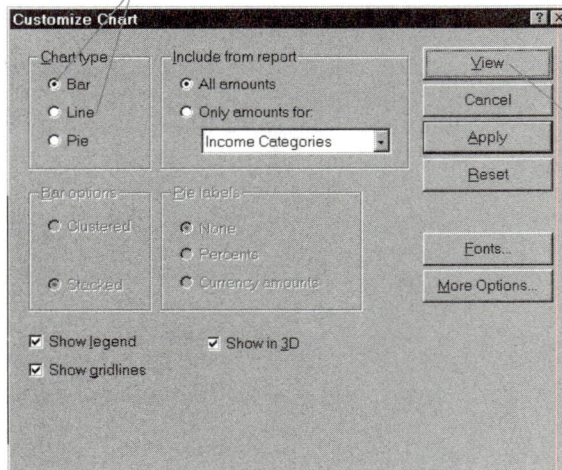

3 Click
here

Customising charts (3)

Applying a new typeface/type size

Generate a standard chart (see pages 117-118), then follow step 1 on page 120. Now carry out steps 1-4 below, as appropriate. Finally, perform step 5 to view the report:

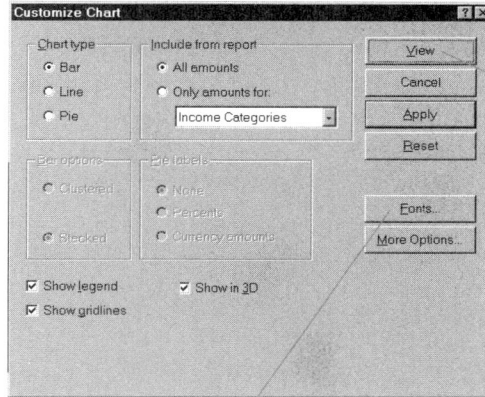

5 Click here

| Click here

2 Click a font

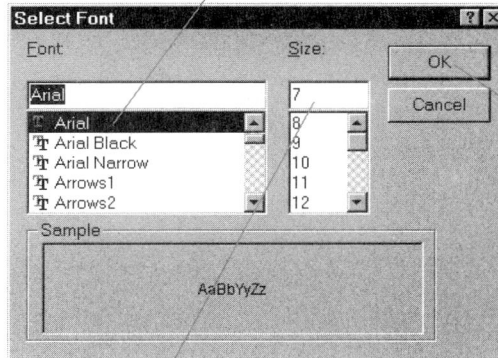

4 Click here

3 Enter a type size

Customising charts (4)

Specifying which transactions are included (A)

Generate a standard chart (see pages 117-118). Follow step 1 on page 120. Carry out steps 1 and 2 below, and then 3 and 4 on page 123. Finally, perform steps 5 and 6 to view the chart:

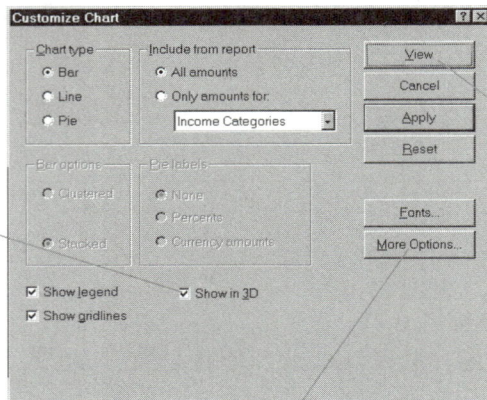

HANDY TIP

By default, Money displays and print charts in 3D.

If you don't want this, deselect this field:

HANDY TIP

To have rows sorted by amount (rather than alphabetically), click here:

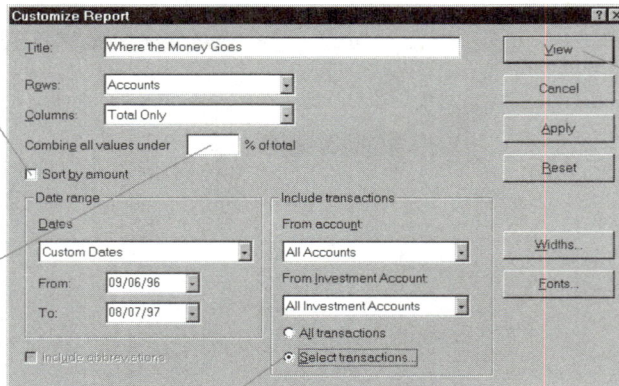

HANDY TIP

To have low-value entries combined into one, enter a percentage of the total value here: (e.g. to lump together entries below £250 in an account whose maximum amount is £5000, enter 5%).

Customize Chart

Chart type
- Bar
- Line
- Pie

Include from report
- All amounts
- Only amounts for:
  Income Categories

View
Cancel
Apply
Reset

6 Click here

Bar options
- Clustered
- Stacked

Pie labels
- None
- Percents
- Currency amounts

Fonts...
More Options...

Show legend
Show gridlines
Show in 3D

Click here

Customize Report

Title: Where the Money Goes
Rows: Accounts
Columns: Total Only
Combing all values under [ ] % of total
Sort by amount

View
Cancel
Apply
Reset

5 Click here

Date range
Dates
Custom Dates
From: 09/06/96
To: 08/07/97

Include transactions
From account
All Accounts
From Investment Account:
All Investment Accounts
- All transactions
- Select transactions...

Include abbreviations

Widths...
Fonts...

2 Click here

Customising charts (5)

Specifying which transactions are included (ß)
carry out the following steps after 1 and 2 on page 122:

3 Type in text to have the report
limited to fields which contain it

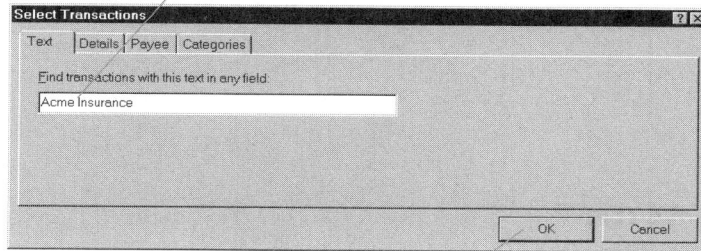

Select Transactions

| Text | Details | Payee | Categories |

Find transactions with this text in any field:

Acme Insurance

OK   Cancel

4 Click here

Other suggestions...
You can use step 3 to apply a variety of additional restrictions:

- to limit the chart to specific transaction types, click the Details tab. Click the Transaction type arrow; in the list, click a type. Now follow steps 3 and 4.

- to limit the chart to specific payees, click the Payee tab. Click the Selected payees field; in the list, click 1 or more payees. Now follow steps 3 and 4.

- to limit the chart to specific categories, click the Categories tab. Click Selected categories; in the list, click 1 or more categories. Now follow steps 3 and 4.

Finally, carry out step 4 above, and then steps 5 and 6 on page 122.

Customising charts (6)

Other changes...

Generate a standard chart (see pages 117-118), then follow step 1 on page 120. Now carry out step 1 below, then any of steps 2-7 as appropriate. Finally, perform steps 8 and 9 to view the report:

9 Click here

HANDY TIP

Re step 7 – if you want to limit the report to *more than one* account, click Multiple Accounts in the list which appears. Now do the following:

2 Click the relevant accounts

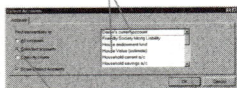

1 Click here **3** Click here

Finally, carry out step 8.

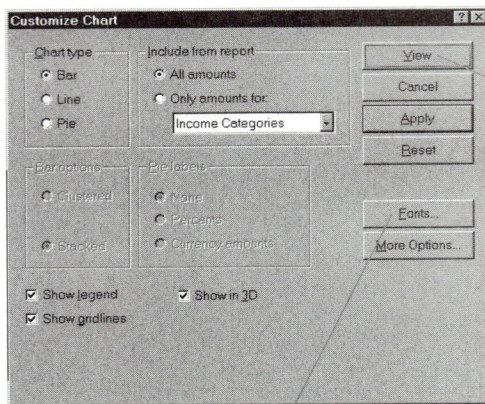

1 Click here

2 Name the report

3 Click here; choose a row basis

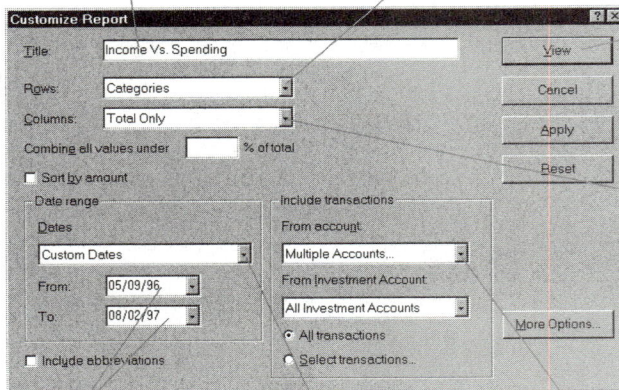

8 Click here

4 Click here; click a column heading

6 Type in start and end dates

5 Click here; click a date range

7 Click here; select an account

Working with charts

When you've created a chart, you can:

- make a chart component display its associated numerical value (complete with additional information, where appropriate, e.g. details of the associated account)

- edit chart components directly

Producing a component display

After you've created a chart, move the mouse pointer over a chart component. The mouse pointer changes to either of the following:

The cross in the first pointer indicates that the component currently selected is directly editable – see 'Direct editing' below.

and Money produces an explanatory box:

```
Mary-retirement (Contributions)
Tax - John
£0.00
```

Direct editing

You can also use the direct editing technique with reports.

After you've created a chart, move the mouse pointer over a chart component. If the mouse pointer changes to:

double-click to produce the appropriate dialog or account.

For example, double-clicking chart dates produces the Customize Report dialog (see steps 5 and 6 on page 124 for how to use this to specify a restrictive date range).

Chart printing

Once you've generated and/or customised a report, you can print it out.

Printing a chart

Pull down the File menu and do the following:

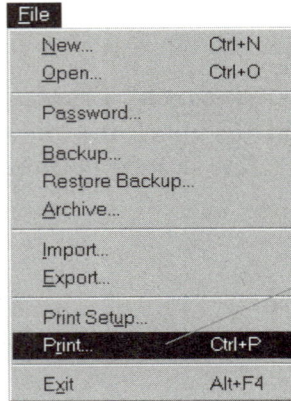

File	
New...	Ctrl+N
Open...	Ctrl+O
Password...	
Backup...	
Restore Backup...	
Archive...	
Import...	
Export...	
Print Setup...	
Print...	Ctrl+P
Exit	Alt+F4

Click here

HANDY TIP

If you need to adjust your printer's internal settings, click the Setup button:

Setup...

Then follow steps 1-4 (as appropriate) on page 115.

3 Click here

Print Chart ? X

Printer: System Printer (Epson Stylus COLOR ESC/P 2)

OK

Cancel

Setup...

Copies: 1

REMEMBER

Re step 2 – the available quality options depend on the selected printer.

Print quality: 180 dpi

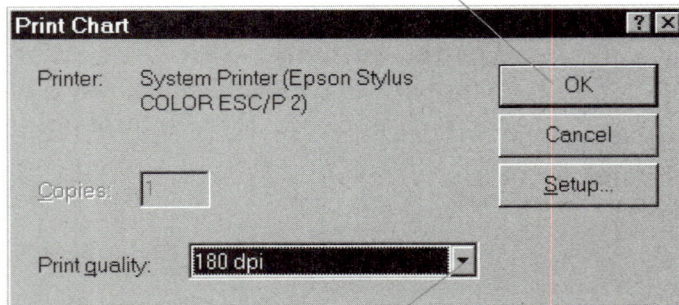

2 Click here; select a print quality in the list

Planning Wizards

Money supplies a series of Wizards to lead you through various financial planning tasks (Wizards simplify complex tasks and make them easy and convenient). Use this chapter to learn how to use them.

Covers

Planning Wizards – an overview 128

Running the Mortgage Planner 129

Running the Retirement Planner 136

Running the Savings Calculator 140

Planning Wizards – an overview

To help you accomplish the most frequently undertaken financial planning tasks, Money comes with several useful wizards:

REMEMBER

In this section, we'll concentrate on the Mortgage Planner, Retirement Planner and Savings Calculator Wizards.
To use either of the remaining Wizards, follow step 1 on page 129. In the Planning Wizards screen, click the button which relates to the relevant Wizard. Then follow the on-screen instructions.

Loan Calculator

Money defines loans as major, long-term debts involving regular payments. Use the Loan Calculator to:

- explore loan alternatives

- calculate interest

- compare loans

- calculate interest reductions due to early payment

Mortgage Planner

When you're planning to take out a mortgage, use the Mortgage Planner to decide which of two offers involving the same amount is best.

Savings Calculator

Use the Savings Calculator to structure your saving, or plan for future spending

Retirement Planner

Use the Retirement Planner to work out how much you'll need to save – and how often – to meet a specific retirement objective

Interest Estimator

Use the Interest Estimator to calculate earned interest for bank accounts, or the amount of interest paid on credit card accounts

Running the Mortgage Planner (1)

In the Contents area, do the following:

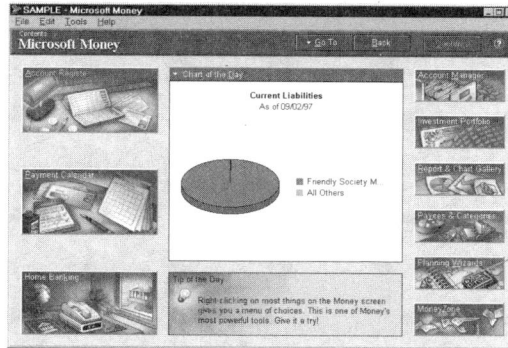

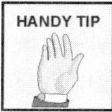 **HANDY TIP**

Press Esc at any time to terminate the Mortgage Planner Wizard. Then do the following:

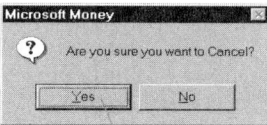

Click here

Click here

Carry out the following steps:

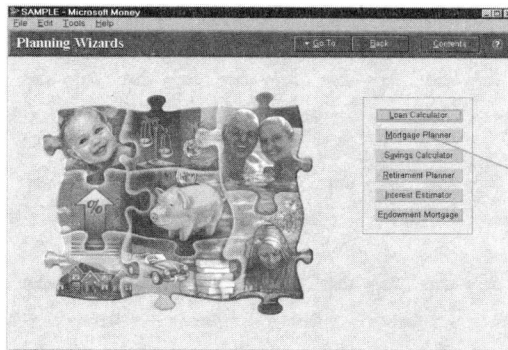

2 Click here

 **HANDY TIP**

Here, the Mortgage Planner compares two offers from the following perspectives:
- **the initial outlay**
- **the monthly payment**
- **the mortgage duration**

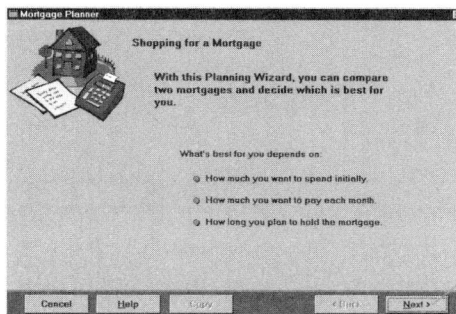

3 Click here

Running the Mortgage Planner (2)

Now carry out the following steps:

Type in the purchase price

Mortgage Planner

What is the purchase price of the property?

Purchase Price: 93,250

The purchase price is the amount you will agree to pay for the property. You'll use this same purchase price to compare two different mortgages.

- Do not include any closing costs or fees in this amount.
- Do not subtract the down payment from this amount.

Cancel   Help   Copy   < Back   Next >

2 Click here

3 Enter the down-payment for the first offer

HANDY TIP

Re steps 3 and 4 – you can enter down-payments as a percentage of the purchase price, or as a specific amount.

Mortgage Planner

For each mortgage, enter the down payment as a percentage of the purchase price or as a fixed amount.

	Mortgage A	Mortgage B
Purchase Price:	93,250.00	93,250.00
Down Payment:	5%	5%
	10%	10%
	Other %:	Other %:
	Amount:	Amount:

A deposit amount of 10, 20, or 30% is typical.

Cancel   Help   Copy   < Back   Next >

4 Enter the down-payment for the second offer

5 Click here

Running the Mortgage Planner (3)

Carry out the following steps:

Money has calculated
the Mortgage amount...

Based on the purchase price and down payment,
here's the mortgage amount for each.

	Mortgage A	Mortgage B
Purchase Price:	93,250.00	93,250.00
– Down Payment:	4,662.50	9,325.00
= Mortgage Amount:	88,587.50	83,925.00

If you want to make changes, click Back.

Cancel   Help   Copy   < Back   Next >

| Click here

2 Ensure these show: 0.00

Enter the balloon amounts, if any.

A balloon amount is a large payment due at the end of the loan.

	Mortgage A	Mortgage B
Purchase Price:	93,250.00	93,250.00
Down Payment:	4,662.50	9,325.00
Mortgage Amount:	88,587.50	83,925.00
Balloon Amount:	0.00	0.00

Most home mortgages do not have balloon payments. If
you're unsure, leave it zero.

Cancel   Help   Copy   < Back   Next >

3 Click here

Running the Mortgage Planner (4)

Now carry out the following steps:

| Enter the length and interest rate for the first offer

BEWARE

Re step 1 – enter the *simple* interest rate...

Mortgage Planner window:

Enter the mortgage length and interest rate for each mortgage.

Be sure to enter the Simple Interest Rate, not the Annual Percentage Rate (APR). Your lender can provide this information.

	Mortgage A	Mortgage B
Mortgage Length:	30 Years	25 Years
Interest Rate:	7 %	7 %

☐ Canadian Mortgages — In Canada, interest on mortgages is often compounded two times per year. Check this option if you're exploring loans of this type.

Cancel Help Copy < Back Next >

2 Enter the length and interest rate for the second offer

3 Click here

4 Ensure these show: 0

Mortgage Planner window:

For each mortgage, enter the fees the lender is charging.

Points are sometimes referred to as a loan origination fee. Generally, if you pay more in points, you get a lower interest rate.(Note: UK lenders do not make points charges)

	Mortgage A	Mortgage B
Points:	0 %	0 %

One point (1.0) is equal to one percent of the mortgage amount. (Note: UK lenders do not make these types of charge)

Cancel Help Copy < Back Next >

5 Click here

Running the Mortgage Planner (5)

Carry out the following steps:

1 Enter the service fee for the first offer

2 Enter the service fee for the second offer

3 Click here

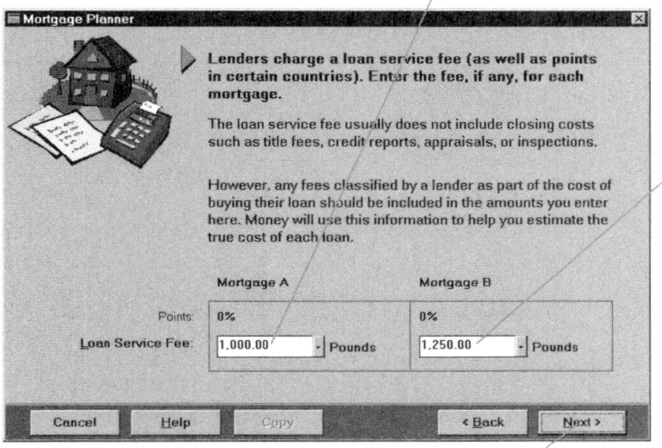

4 Enter the closing costs for the first offer

5 Enter the closing costs for the second offer

6 Click here

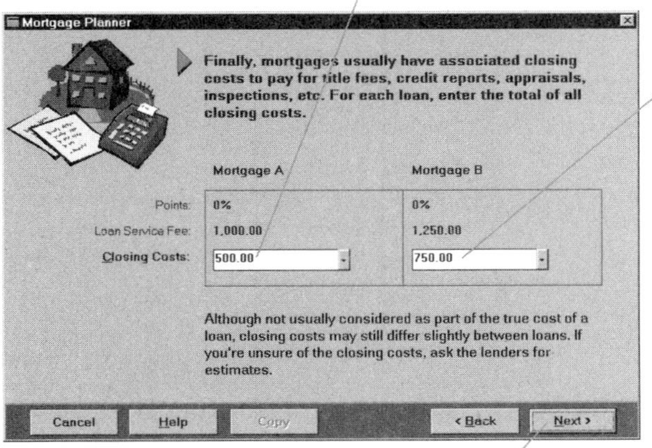

Running the Mortgage Planner (6)

Carry out the following additional steps:

Money has calculated
the initial costs

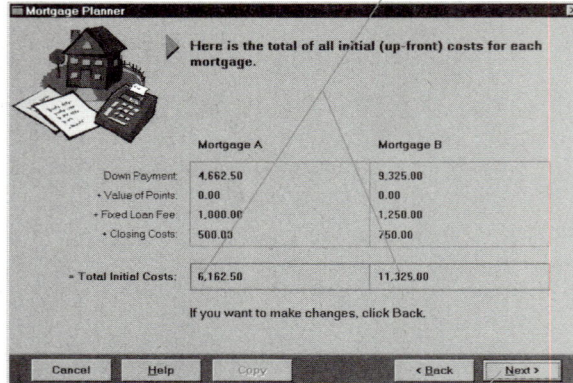

Mortgage Planner

▷ Here is the total of all initial (up-front) costs for each mortgage.

	Mortgage A	Mortgage B
Down Payment:	4,662.50	9,325.00
• Value of Points:	0.00	0.00
+ Fixed Loan Fee:	1,000.00	1,250.00
+ Closing Costs:	500.00	750.00
= Total Initial Costs:	6,162.50	11,325.00

If you want to make changes, click Back.

| Cancel | Help | Copy | < Back | Next > |

Click here

Money now begins to draw comparisons between the offers:

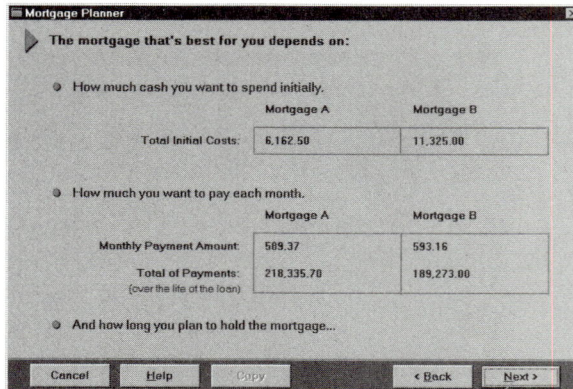

Mortgage Planner

▷ The mortgage that's best for you depends on:

● How much cash you want to spend initially.

	Mortgage A	Mortgage B
Total Initial Costs:	6,162.50	11,325.00

● How much you want to pay each month.

	Mortgage A	Mortgage B
Monthly Payment Amount:	509.37	593.16
Total of Payments: (over the life of the loan)	218,335.70	189,273.00

● And how long you plan to hold the mortgage...

| Cancel | Help | Copy | < Back | Next > |

Here, Money
compares the
offers on two
grounds:
* initial
  payment
* monthly
  spending

2 Click here

Running the Mortgage Planner (7)

And now for the third comparison:

Only carry out steps 1 and 2 if you intend to terminate the mortgage before its natural expiry.

In step 1, insert the period for which you intend to retain the mortgage.

After step 2, Money displays the result here:

Here, Money compares the APR for the two offers

Type in a hold period

2 Click here

3 Click here

To print a copy of the summary, click the Copy button in the final dialog. In your word processor, carry out the appropriate Paste (usually Shift+Insert) and Print (usually Ctrl+P) commands.

Click the Done button to close the Wizard:

Finally, Money summarises the offers and calculates the difference

Running the Retirement Planner (1)

In the Contents area, do the following:

HANDY TIP

The Retirement Planner assumes **you'll be making consistent monthly payments into your retirement plan.**

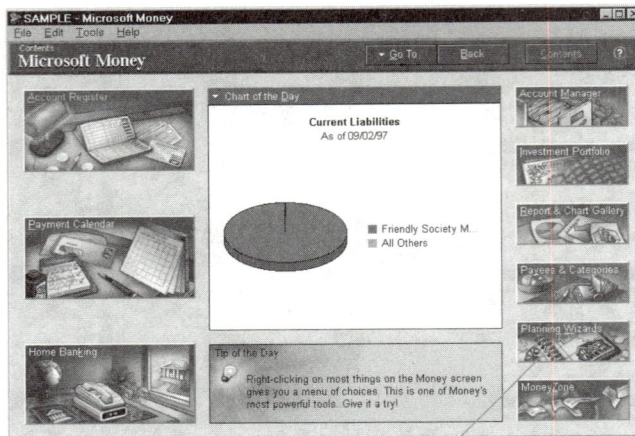

Click here

Carry out the following:

HANDY TIP

The Retirement Planner can adjust **its projections to obviate the effects of inflation – an extremely useful feature.**

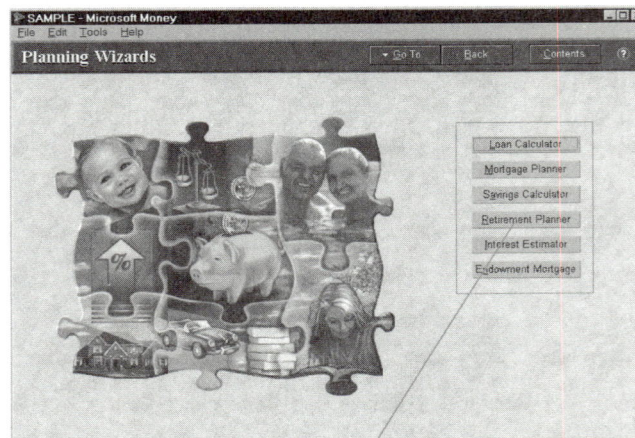

2 Click here

Running the Retirement Planner (2)

Carry out the following steps to utilise the Retirement Planner:

HANDY TIP

Re step 1 – if in any doubt, over-estimate your life expectancy (to compensate for larger-than-expected increases in inflation).

Complete these fields

2 Click here

3 Type in the monthly figure you want to achieve

HANDY TIP

Press Esc at any time to terminate the Retirement Planner. Then do the following:

4 Type in your current retirement savings

Click here

5 Click here

Running the Retirement Planner (3)

Carry out the following additional steps:

1 Type in your retirement interest as a %

REMEMBER

Re step 1 – enter a *cautious* estimate, after taxes have been allowed for.

Retirement Planner

What is the current return on your retirement savings?

Your return is the total of all interest, dividends, or other gains you receive on savings and other investments, expressed as an annual percentage. Enter a conservative value that estimates your return after taxes.

Pre-Retirement Return: [ ] % Annually

After you retire, what return will you expect from your savings?

On reaching retirement, you may decide to move your savings to lower-risk investments which have lower yields, like National Savings Certificates or Government Stocks (Gilts).

Post-Retirement Return: [6] % Annually

Cancel   Help   Copy   < Back   Next >

2 Type in your *expected* return (after retirement) as a %

3 Click here

REMEMBER

Re step 4 – by default, Money assumes an inflation rate of 3% and bases the post-inflation summary on this.
To change this, type in a new rate, then click here: Finally, carry out step 5.

4 Type in the expected inflation rate

Retirement Planner

Adjustment For Inflation

Inflation may cause the money you save today to be worth less by the time you retire. You can keep up with inflation by increasing the amount of your contributions.

Money will revise your goal to compensate for inflation, and use these new values in its calculations on the following pages.

Annual Inflation Rate: [3] %

Calculate

Your Original Goal (Ignoring Inflation):

▷ 750.00 monthly retirement income from age 65 to 85.

▷ Your total savings at age 65 would need to be 106,038.23.

Revised Goal (Assuming 3% inflation):

▷ 1,820.45 monthly retirement income at age 65, increasing with inflation to 3,287.93 at age 85.

▷ Your total savings at age 65 would need to be 331,179.47.

Cancel   Help   Copy   < Back   Next >

A summary of your retirement objectives...

The summary updated to include inflation

5 Click here

Running the Retirement Planner (4)

In the next dialog, Money compares the effects of:

- uniform retirement contributions

- incrementing retirement contributions

Carry out the following steps:

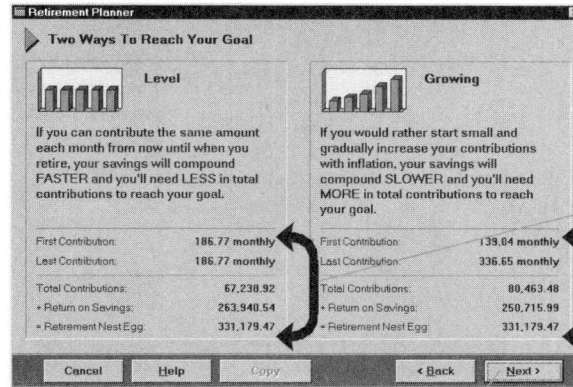

Compare the two

Click here

Money now generates a report. Do the following:

HANDY TIP **To print a copy of the report, click the Copy button. Open your word processor; carry out the appropriate Paste (usually Shift+Insert) and Print (usually Ctrl+P) commands.**

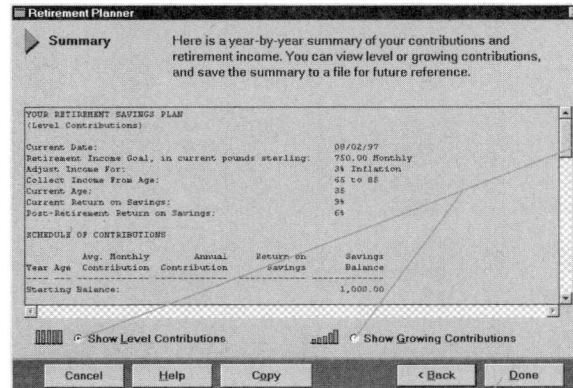

2 Click a savings method to vary the report

3 Click here

Running the Savings Calculator

**Re step 1 –
you can
leave any 1
field blank**

HANDY TIP

**Re step 1 –
you can
leave any 1
field blank
to have Money
complete it from the
information
supplied in the
other fields...**

In the Contents area, follow step 1 on page 136. In the
Planning Wizard screen, click:

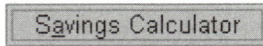

| Savings Calculator |

Now carry out the following steps:

HANDY TIP

**Step 3 is
optional –
follow it if
you want
your savings plan to
take account of
inflation.**

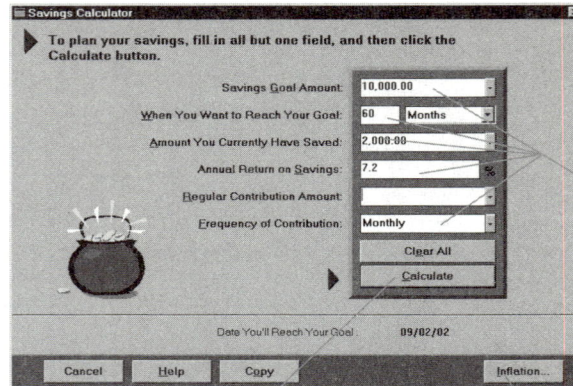

Savings Calculator

To plan your savings, fill in all but one field, and then click the
Calculate button.

Savings Goal Amount:	10,000.00
When You Want to Reach Your Goal:	60	Months
Amount You Currently Have Saved:	2,000.00
Annual Return on Savings:	7.2	%
Regular Contribution Amount:	
Frequency of Contribution:	Monthly

Clear All

Calculate

Date You'll Reach Your Goal: 09/02/02

Cancel   Help   Copy   Inflation...

1 Complete
all fields
bar one

2 Click here

3 Click here

HANDY TIP

**By default,
Money
assumes
an
inflation rate of 3%;
the figures here:
reflect this.**

**To explore the
effect of changing
the inflation rate,
follow step 4.
Finally, carry out
step 5 to return to
the original savings
details. Or, to close
the Wizard, press
Esc; in the message
which launches,
click Yes.**

Savings Calculator

Effect of Inflation

Inflation will reduce the purchasing
power of the money you save.

- In your case, the 10,000.00 you're saving
will be worth 8,626.09 in 5 Years, assuming
a 3 % inflation rate.

- To compensate for inflation, you may want
to increase your monthly contribution from
100.20 to 122.46 pounds.

- This means you'll save more than you
originally planned, but the higher amount
will be worth 10,000.00 pounds AFTER
inflation.

Your Original Plan

Total Amount Saved:	10,000.00
Value in Today's terms:	8,626.09
Regular Contribution:	100.20

Revised Plan (For Inflation)

Total Amount Saved:	11,592.74
Value in Today's Pounds:	10,000.00
Regular Contribution:	122.46

Annual Inflation Rate:
3 % Calculate

Cancel   Help   Copy   < Back

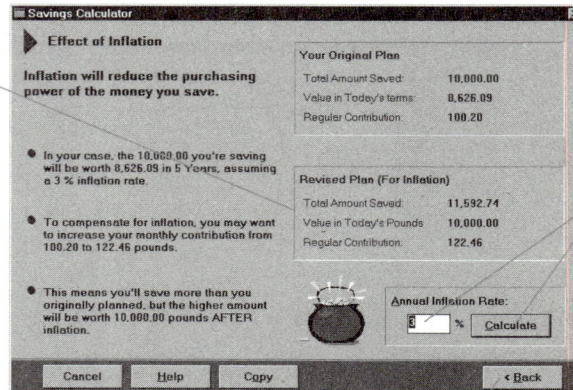

4 Type in a
new
inflation
rate and
click
Calculate

5 Click here

Home Banking

Use this chapter to learn how to make use of Money's inbuilt online banking facilities. First, you'll allocate a bank to your accounts. Then you'll 'sign up', an essential preliminary. Finally, you'll pay bills electronically; transfer funds between accounts; send online letters; and have Money update your accounts automatically.

Covers

Home Banking – an overview 142

Preparing to sign up 143

Signing up for Online Services 145

Paying bills electronically 150

Electronic account transfers 152

Writing to Online Services 153

Updating your account 154

Home Banking – an overview

REMEMBER **You can have Money pay** *recurring* **bills electronically, too (providing your bank supports this).**
   Follow steps 1-7 on pages 76-77 (but also type 'Apay' – without the quotes – in the Number field). Click the Go To button in the overhead Navigation Bar; select Home Banking. Finally, carry out steps 2-3 on page 151.

If you have a modem connected to your PC, you can use Money's in-built Home Banking feature to:

- pay bills electronically

- carry out online banking tasks. These include:

  - updating your accounts electronically

  - transferring funds between accounts electronically

  - writing to your bank

- connect to the MoneyZone (see Section 1 for how to do this)

Caveats

You should bear in mind the following:

- currently, few banks in the UK offer online banking

- banks which do provide online banking offer varying services, and may not supply all of the services listed above

- you should contact your bank *before* you attempt to use Money's online banking. You need the following information:

  - your bank's URL (Internet address)

  - the identification code provided by your bank

  - other standard bank information (e.g. your bank account number and sort code)

BEWARE **You can't print out cheques in Money.**
You can only:
- **continue to write them by hand**
OR
- **send them electronically**

before you can establish the necessary connection by 'signing up'.

Preparing to sign up (1)

You need to perform the following preliminary actions before you can proceed with the signing up process:

1. Contact your bank to find out if it offers online banking facilities

2. If it does, find out:

    – your bank's URL (Internet address)

    – the identification code provided by your bank

    – other standard bank information (e.g. your bank account number and sort code)

3. Assign your bank to the relevant account(s)

Assigning your bank

In the Contents area, do the following:

REMEMBER **You won't need to carry out this procedure if you inserted the bank details when you set up the account.**

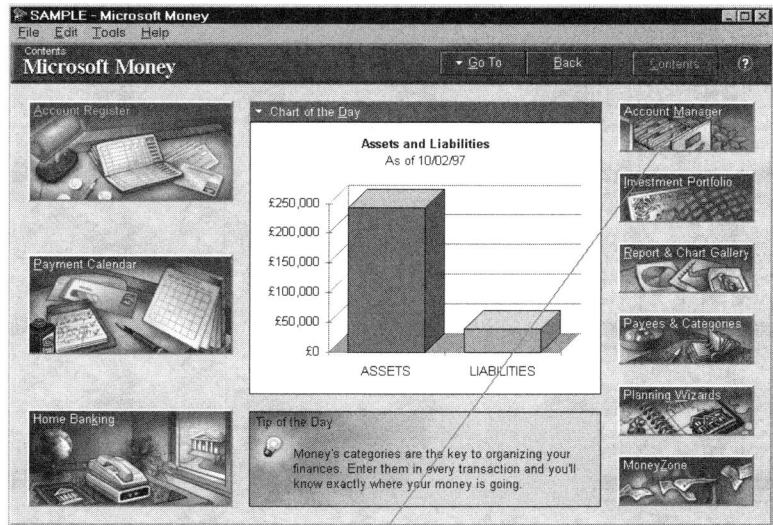

Click here

Preparing to sign up (2)

To complete the assigning process, do the following:

| Click an account

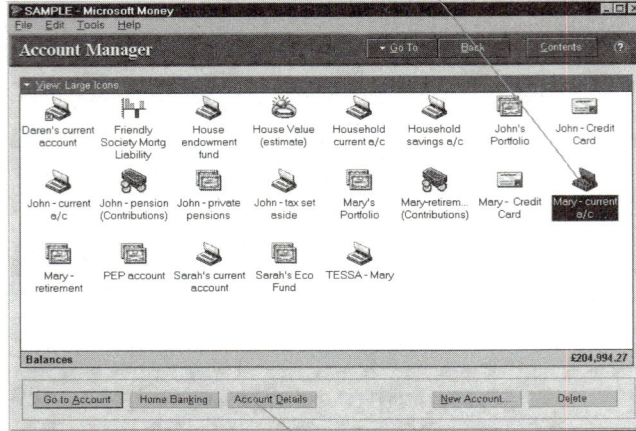

REMEMBER

Re step 3 – if the Bank name field already shows the name of your bank, you can ignore the procedures on this page. Go to page 145.

2 Click here

HANDY TIP

If you proceed with step 3 when a different bank has previously been allocated, a special message appears. Do the following:

Click here to update all associated accounts

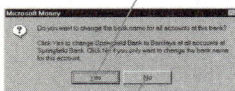

Click here to update only the one account

3 Type in the bank's name and press Enter

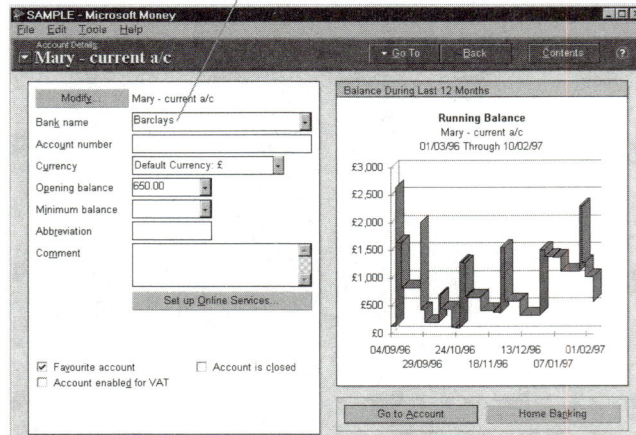

Signing up for Online Services (1)

In Money's Contents area, do the following:

After following the procedures on pages 143 and 144, you're now ready to begin the signing up process...

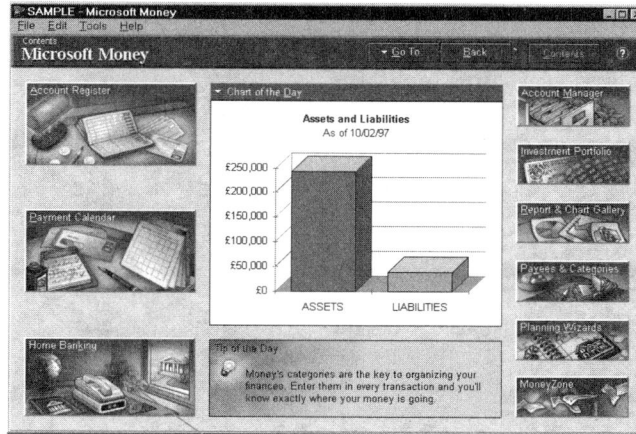

Click here

In the Home Banking area, carry out the following steps:

2 Click here; select an online bank

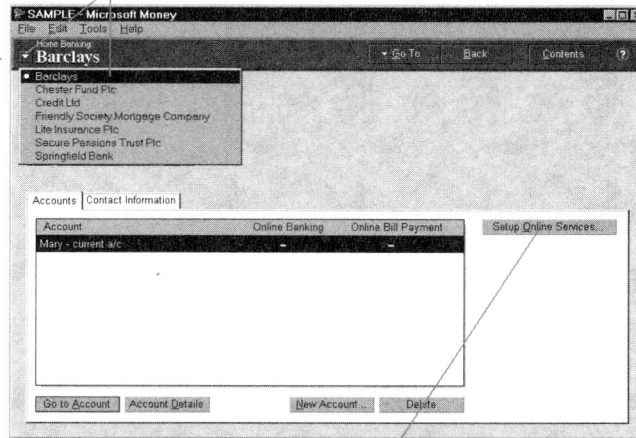

3 Click here

Signing up for Online Services (2)

Carry out the following steps:

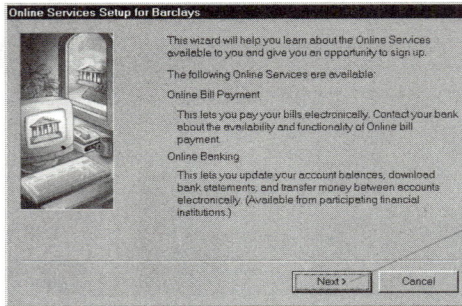

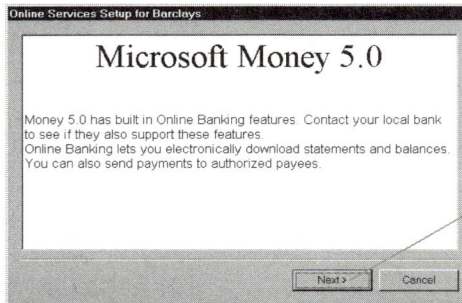

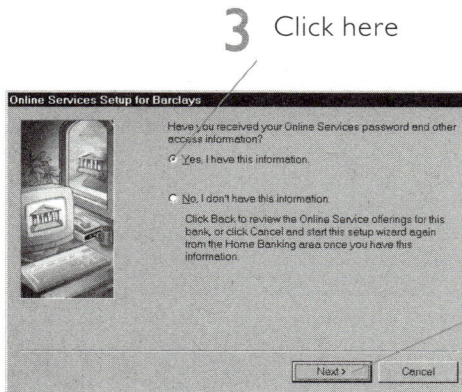

Online Services Setup for Barclays

This wizard will help you learn about the Online Services available to you and give you an opportunity to sign up.

The following Online Services are available:

Online Bill Payment

This lets you pay your bills electronically. Contact your bank about the availability and functionality of Online bill payment.

Online Banking

This lets you update your account balances, download bank statements, and transfer money between accounts electronically. (Available from participating financial institutions.)

Next >   Cancel

1 Click here

Online Services Setup for Barclays

Microsoft Money 5.0

Money 5.0 has built in Online Banking features. Contact your local bank to see if they also support these features.
Online Banking lets you electronically download statements and balances. You can also send payments to authorized payees.

Next >   Cancel

2 Click here

---

3 Click here

Online Services Setup for Barclays

Have you received your Online Services password and other access information?

○ Yes, I have this information.

○ No, I don't have this information.

Click Back to review the Online Service offerings for this bank, or click Cancel and start this setup wizard again from the Home Banking area once you have this information.

Next >   Cancel

4 Click here

Signing up for Online Services (3)

To continue with the signing up process, do the following:

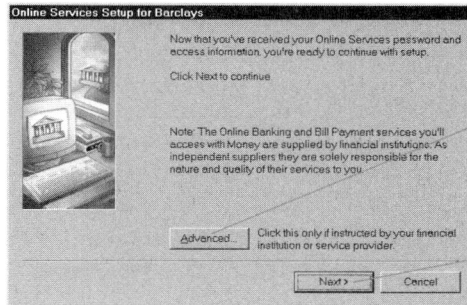

| Click here

5 Click here

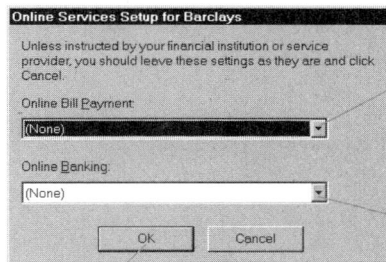

2 Click here; select a payment method

3 Click here; select a banking method

4 Click here

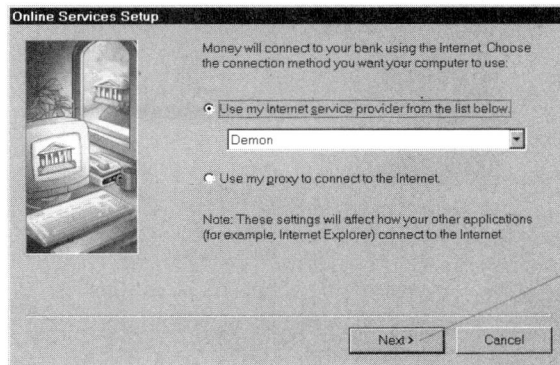

6 Click here

Signing up for Online Services (4)

HANDY TIP

Re step 1 – URL stands for Uniform Resource Locator. URLs are unique addresses for World Wide Web sites.

If you need more information on the Internet, consider buying 'Internet UK in easy steps'.

Carry out the following steps:

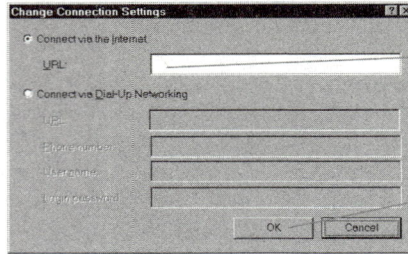

1 Enter your bank's URL

2 Click here

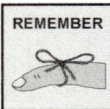
REMEMBER

After step 2, Money launches a special message. Do the following:

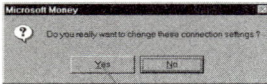

Click here

Now carry out steps 3-6.

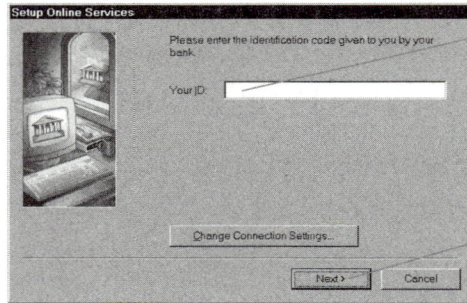

3 Enter your identification code

4 Click here

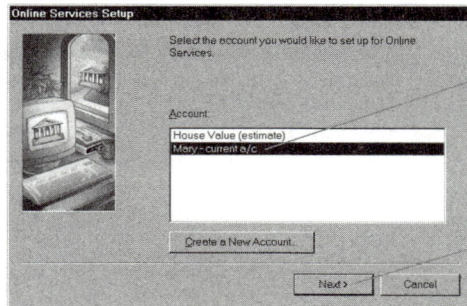

5 Click an account

6 Click here

Signing up for Online Services (5)

To finalise the signing up process, do the following:

1 Complete these fields

2 Click here

3 Click here

4 Click here

REMEMBER

Step 5 completes the signing up process.

Now you can:
- **pay bills electronically**
- **transfer funds between accounts electronically**
- **draft letters to Online Services**
- **update your accounts electronically**

5 Click here

Paying bills electronically (1)

In the Account Register, do the following:

Click here

HANDY TIP

Re step 2 – accounts which are online-enabled have:

against them.

2 Click the relevant account

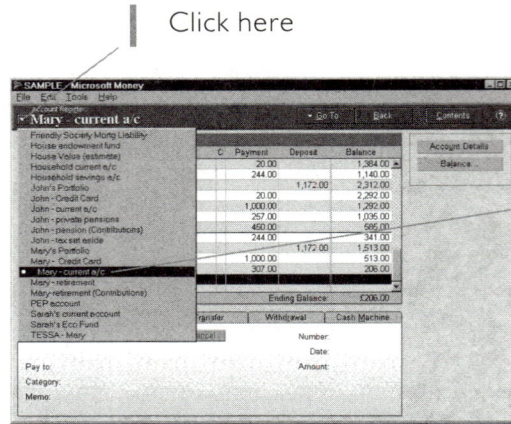

Re step 4 – insert 'Epay' (minus the quote marks) in the Number field.

REMEMBER

In the Register form, do the following:

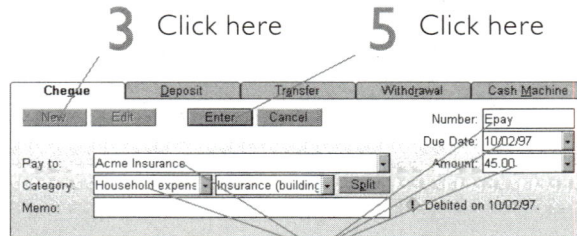

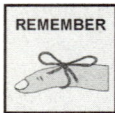

3 Click here   5 Click here

| Cheque | Deposit | Transfer | Withdrawal | Cash Machine |

| New | Edit | Enter | Cancel | Number: Epay |
Due Date: 10/02/97

Pay to: Acme Insurance
Amount: 45.00
Category: Household expens ▾ Insurance (building ▾ Split
Memo: ‡ Debited on 10/02/97.

4 Complete the necessary fields

After step 5, Money launches a special message. Do the following:

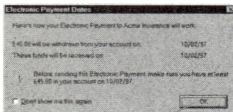

REMEMBER

The illustration below shows the inserted transaction:

This icon indicates that the transaction is pending: it will be sent the next time you connect to Online Services (see page 151)

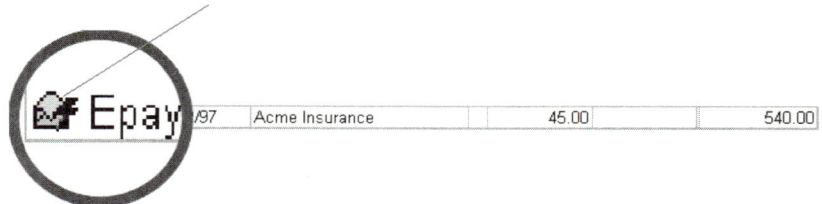

Click here

Epay   /97   Acme Insurance   45.00   540.00

Paying bills electronically (2)

HANDY TIP

After creating an electronic transaction (and/or carrying out any of the procedures on pages 152 & 153), it's now time to send it...

To begin transmission, do the following in the Contents area:

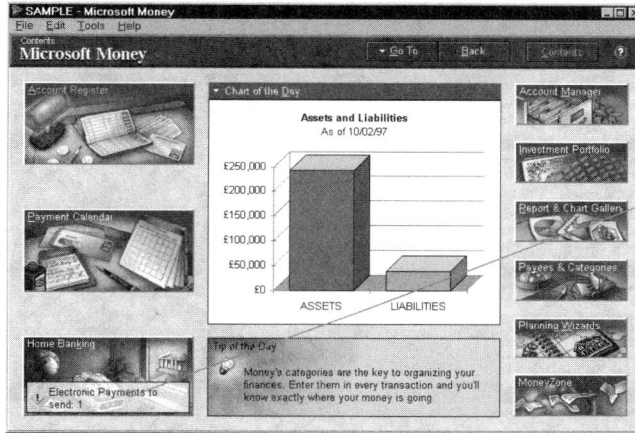

Click here

HANDY TIP

Re step 1 – if you're still in the Account Register, you can use an alternative route to launch the Home Banking area. A special message appears near the form. Do the following:

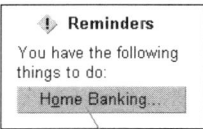

> **Reminders**
> You have the following things to do:
> [Home Banking...]

Click here

Now follow steps 2 and 3 below.

Now carry out the following steps in the Home Banking area:

2 Ensure the Connect tab is activated

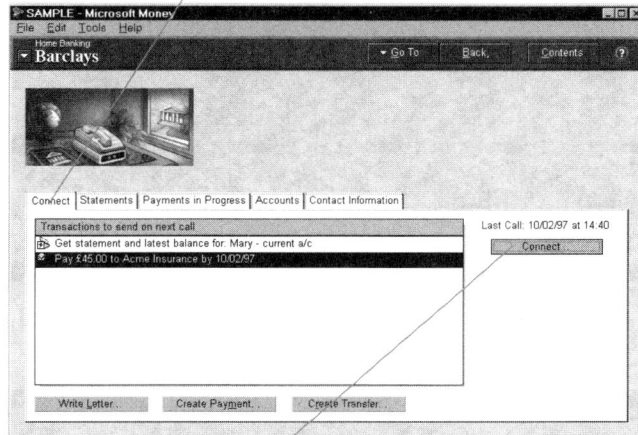

3 Click here and follow the on-screen instructions

Electronic account transfers

To transfer funds between accounts, do the following in the Account Register:

Click here

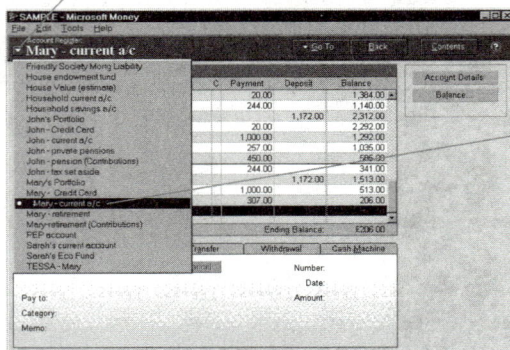

2 Click the relevant account

REMEMBER

Re step 4 – insert 'Xfer' (minus the quote marks) in the Number field.

In the Register form, do the following:

5 Click here   3 Click here

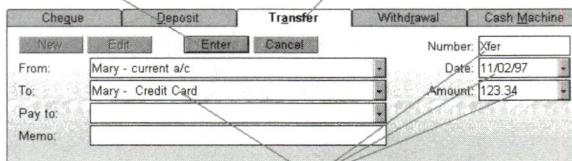

4 Complete the necessary fields

The next stage is to transmit your transaction electronically. To do this, follow the procedures on page 151.

Writing to Online Services

To write to Online Services, click:

in the Contents area. Now do the following:

| Click here

2 Click here

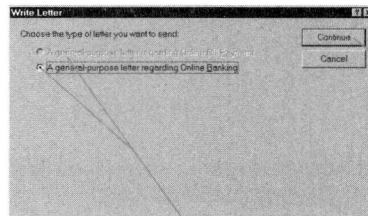

4 Click here

3 Click one of these

5 Click here; select an account

REMEMBER
After step 7, follow the procedures on page 151 to send your letter.

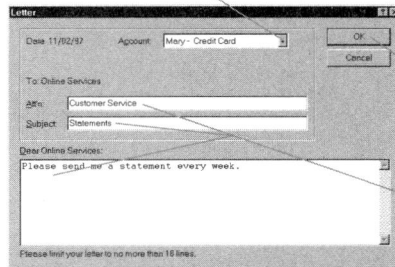

7 Click here

6 Complete these fields

Updating your account

Connecting to Online Services is a two-way process: you can also download transactions directly from your bank. This means that you no longer need to enter manually cashpoint withdrawals, deposits and handwritten cheques.

In the Account Register, do the following:

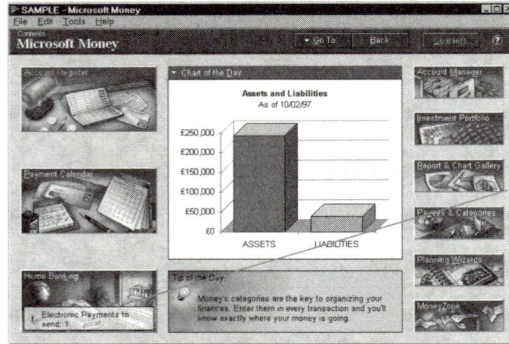

Click here

Follow steps 2 and 3 on page 151. Then carry out the following steps:

2 Click this tab

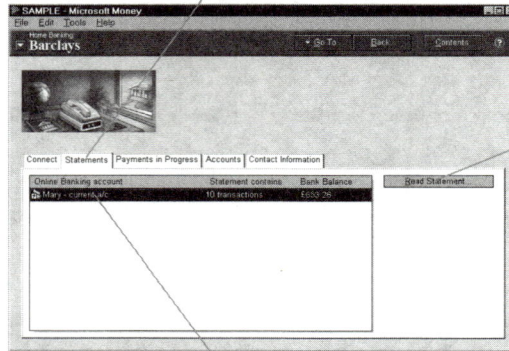

4 Click here

REMEMBER

After this, Money displays the first downloaded transaction in a special form. Click Next to ratify it. Repeat this for all transactions.

3 Click an account with unread transactions

Click Update Account Register. Then see the Remember tip on the left.

Index

A

Account Manager   59
Accounts   57-72
  Automatic balance totalling   60
  Balance Account side-bar   91, 95-100
  Closing   66
  Creating   60-62
  Defined   24
  Deleting   67
  Editing   64-65
  Favourites, marking/viewing   64
  Launching the Account Manager   59
  Opening   63
  Overview   58
  Printing   72
  Reconciling. *See* Reconciliation
  Register   37-56
  Renaming   65
  Transactions. *See* Transactions
  Transferring transactions
    between   68-69
Archiving files   31-32
AutoComplete, turning off   41
AutoReconcile   100-101

B

Backups   27-28
Balance Account side-bar   91, 95-100
Balance Forecaster Graph   106
Banks
  Online Services   141-154
  Statements   85, 102
Bills, paying electronically   150-151

C

Calendar   74-75, 83
Categories
  Amending   52
  Applying   45
  Creating   46
  Overview   44
  Printing lists of   72
  Vs. sub-categories   44
Charts   117-126
  Chart of the Day   107
  Creating standard   117-118
  Customising   119-124
    Applying a typeface/type size   121
    Changing the type   120
    Deselecting 3D   122
    Specifying which transactions are
      included   122-123
  Editing data in   125
  Overview   104-105
  Printing   126
  Saving as Favourites   119
  Types of   106-107
  Viewing data in   125
  Viewing Favourites   119
Cheques, Money's inability to print   142
Classifications   48-52
  Amending   52
  Applying items   49
  Applying sub-items   49
  Creating   50-51
  Items/sub-items   48
  Overview   48
  Printing lists of   72
  Vs. categories   48
Contents screen   9

D

Direct debits   73, 83-84

E

Exporting files   33-34

F

Favourites
  Accounts   64
  Charts   119
  Reports   110
Files   23-36
  Archives, creating   31-32
  Backing up   27, 67
    Reminder system,   28
  Creating   25
  Default   26
  Exporting   33-34
    Format types   33
  Importing   35-36
    Format types   35
  Opening   26
  Overview   24
  Restoring after backup   29-30
Find Transactions dialog   43

H

HELP   11-14
  Closing   12-14
  Launching from Contents screen   11
    By right-clicking   14
  Launching from the Help menu   12
  Product Tours   15-17
    Closing   17
    Running   15-17
  Using Contents   12
  Using Find   13
  Using Index   13

Home Banking   141-154
  Assigning banks to accounts   143-144
  Caveats   142
  Overview   142
  Paying bills   150-151
  Preparing to sign up   143-144
  Signing up   145-149
  Transferring funds between
    accounts   152
  Updating accounts   154
  Writing to Online Services   153

I

Importing files   35-36

M

Mine.MNY   24-26
Money screen   9-10
  Contents screen   9
  Navigation bar   9-10
  Specifying start-up screen   9
  Tip area   9
MoneyZone   18-22, 142
  Connecting to   18-20
    From within Money   19
    From within your browser   20
    Requirements   18
  Home page   21
  Using   21-22
Mortgage Planner   129-135

N

Navigation Bar   9-10
New Account Wizard   60-62

O

Online Services   141-154. *See* Home
  Banking

P

Payees, printing lists of   72
Payment Calendar   74-75, 83. *See also*
   Transactions: Scheduled
  Launching   75
  Scheduled transaction reminders
   in   80
  Using the Balance Forecaster Graph
   in   106
  Using the calendar in   83
Planning Wizards   127-140
  Mortgage Planner   129-135
   Closing   129
   Printing the final summary   135
   Running   129-135
  Others   128
  Overview   128
  Retirement Planner   136-139
   Closing   137
   Printing the final report   139
  Savings Calculator   140
Product Tours   15-17. *See also* HELP:
  Product Tours

Q

QIF (Quicken Interchange Format) files
  Exporting to   33-34
  Importing from   35-36

R

Reconciliation   85-102
  Balance Account side-bar   91, 95-100
  Completing if not
   straightforward   102
  Completing if straightforward   96
  Defined   86
  Initial   87
  Overview   86-87

Resolving discrepancies   97-102
  By inserting transactions   98-99
  By revising transactions   98-99
  By using AutoReconcile   100-101
  Overview   97
  With automatic balancing   102
Register   37-56
  Defined   24
  Making the form visible   39
Reminders   80-82
Reports   104-116
  Creating standard   108-109
  Customising   110-114
   Applying a typeface/type size   112
   Changing column widths   113
   Specifying which transactions
   display   114
  Overview   104-105
  Print setup   115
  Printing   116
  Saving as Favourites   110
  Types of   106-107
  Viewing Favourites   110
Retirement Planner   136-139

S

Sample.MNY   17
Savings Calculator   140
Scheduled transactions. *See*
  Transactions: Scheduled
Screen, elements of   9
Splits
  Adjusting   55-56
  Creating   54
  Overview   53
Standing orders   73, 83-84
Starting Money   8
Sub-categories. *See also* Categories
  Applying   45
  Creating   47

T

Task Bar reminders   81
Transactions
  Deleting/voiding   70-71
  Entering
    Directly   40
    Via the form   39
    With AutoComplete   41
    With shortcuts   42
  Fields listed   38
  Moving between
    With keyboard shortcuts   43
    With the Find Transactions
    dialog   43
  Overview   38
  Scheduled   73-84
    Amending   78-79
    Entering into the Register   83-84
    Reminder systems   80-82
    Setting up   76-77
  Splits. *See* Splits
  Transferring   68-69
  Unvoiding   71

U

URL   148